BREATHING THE PAGE

Breathing the Page
Reading the Act of Writing

Betsy Warland

Cormorant Books

Canada Council **Conseil des Arts**
for the Arts **du Canada**

ONTARIO ARTS COUNCIL
CONSEIL DES ARTS DE L'ONTARIO

The publisher gratefully acknowledges the support of the
Canada Council for the Arts and the Ontario Arts Council
for its publishing program. We acknowledge the financial support
of the Government of Canada through the Book Publishing
Industry Development Program (BPIDP) for our publishing activities.

LIBRARY AND ARCHIVES CANADA CATALOGUING IN PUBLICATION

Warland, Betsy, 1946–
Breathing the page : reading the act of writing / Betsy Warland.

ISBN 978-1-897151-78-5

1. Authorship. 1. Title.

PN145.W37 2010   808'.02   C2009-907181-9

Cover image and design: Angel Guerra/Archetype
Interior text design: Tannice Goddard, Soul Oasis Networking
Printer: Transcontinental

Printed and bound in Canada

FSC

Mixed Sources
Product group from well-managed
forests, controlled sources and
recycled wood or fiber

Cert no. SW-COC-000952
www.fsc.org
© 1996 Forest Stewardship Council

This book is printed on 100% post-consumer waste recycled paper.

CORMORANT BOOKS INC.
215 SPADINA AVENUE, STUDIO 230, TORONTO, ON CANADA M5T 2C7
www.cormorantbooks.com

I dedicate this book to my son Leif Warland Shantz,
who is one of my best and most fascinating teachers.

When in the act of writing, I fully entrust myself to it: place myself willingly in the very midst of the beautiful chaos of meaning unfolding. The terror and joy of this are like none other. Writing is a way of perceiving where everything converges. Which is possibly eternity.

"The Writing Life that Almost Isn't," by Betsy Warland, *Event*, Summer issue 31/2, 2002

Author's Note

My use of the term:

- *narrative* refers to all literary genres;
- *creative non-fiction* refers to all non-fiction and mixed genre writing shaped by literary sensibilities, devices and strategies;
- *subject* refers to topic and/or personage;
- *inscription* refers to the writing of the first draft;
- *composition* refers to the revision and shaping of the first draft to final draft;
- *scoring* refers to how we shape and place a line or sentence on the page;
- *first readers* refers to a selected group of acute readers who read and respond to works prior to the final draft.

Contents

Locating the Reader   1

The Page   10

In-fluencies # 1   13

Memory as Metaphor   14

Quote-tidian # 1   21

Heartwood   24

The Pencil   28

Embodiment   30

Quote-tidian # 2   38

The Alphabet   39

The Coma Story and the Comma Story   43

Quote-tidian # 3   49

Proximity   51

The Line   60

Scaffolding   64

Depth of Field   70

The Table   75

In-fluencies # 2   78

Scored Space   79

Methods of Inscription and Composition   85

Spatiotemporal Structural Strategies   88

In-fluencies # 3   103

Proportion   104

In-fluencies # 4   107

The Written Word   108

Nose to Nose: Poetry   112

Intrinsic Form   117

Territory and Landmarks   128

In-fluencies # 5   133

The Computer   134

The Writing Room   139

Quote-tidian # 4   143

Sustaining Yourself as a Writer   144

Acknowledgements   167

Sources and Resources   170

Other Books by the Author   173

Publication History of Essays   174

Index of Writing Exercises   175

Index of Terms, Phrases, and Images   177

Locating the Reader

Why does it take a while for my reader to become involved in my narrative?

I.

A reader's decision to read a narrative may be a greater act of surrender than a writer's decision to write that narrative. Although a reader may choose to moderate his encounter with the narrative, this can prove to be an illusion. At one time or another, most of us have believed we were reading judiciously, even dismissively, only to discover later that an image, line, or scene from a narrative has taken up residence within us.

The act of reading is an act of belief.

Most readers make the decision to read or not read or discontinue reading within the first seconds or minutes of encountering a text. Like dogs meeting in a park, scents are immediately exchanged; compatibility or lack of it is determined. Acted upon. When the scent is confused, overpowering, or too faint, the reader's interest falters.

For the bond between reader and narrative to flourish, the narrative's opening lines or sentences must signal the reader to a compelling situation that the narrative promises to address. I call this "the predicament." The predicament drives the entire narrative, whether it is a single poem or a book-length prose narrative. The predicament doesn't spell out the whole story, but it cues the reader, signals or gestures what fuels our desire to tell the story — and the reader's desire to read it. A simple device such as an arresting image or phrase, or engaging dialogue, can provide a compelling cue. The predicament may issue from a longing, a problem, a tension, a dilemma, or a puzzle that intrigues the writer, the reader, and the very narrative itself. It functions as a hinge on which the door to the narrative opens to the reader.

Consider the following excerpts from a work-in-progress. In the first excerpt, we encounter how the narrator handles her grief over her mother's death. In the second excerpt, we get a glimpse of the conditions necessitating this narrative (the predicament) in her account of her rather bizarre actions on the heels of her husband's death. There is a sense of stasis (predilection) in the first excerpt. In contrast, her emotional strategies are no longer tenable in the second excerpt. Consequently, our curiosity is incited. We become invested in the narrative: we want to know how will she navigate her way out of her utter disarray.

"After the First Death"
by Leslie Hill

We had picked out a coffin, a plot, a headstone, written the newspaper announcement, *donations to charity in lieu of flowers*, chosen the readings, spoken to the minister. There was little left to do when the time came except confirm the dates and times.

My sister had suggested a piper.

"You want *bagpipes*?" I'd said.

"Why not? She's a McLean; she loves them."

"Yes, well, I love them too, but if you think I can cope with bagpipes at her funeral, think again. I'd go to pieces at a stranger's funeral if there were bagpipes. Absolutely not."

My brother nodded agreement, his eyes bright with grief. My father was silent.

So there were no bagpipes. But it was hard enough. One of my mother's friends came over to the house two days after Mum had died. She burst into tears as she came into the back yard where I was sitting on the steps with a book.

"For God's sake, don't *cry*, Sharon!" I snapped. She straightened up as if I'd slapped her.

"Sorry," she said.

"We have to get through this, and if you cry we'll all cry, so just don't."

"Sorry. I brought you ..." She held out a covered casserole dish and tried to smile.

"Thank you. It'll be a huge relief from my cooking. Is your name on the dish? It's chilly out here. Come inside and have a coffee. Or a drink. Never mind that it's still morning, I'm surviving on sherry."

The sherry would keep me upright and tearless, I thought, as long as other people showed a decent amount of restraint.

The funeral home visits were packed. My father greeted everyone, the ones he knew and those he didn't. Dad never lost his social skills. Two older women who were strangers to me looked at me and burst into tears. I ground my teeth and turned away as my father patted them on the shoulders. Apparently they had known my mother when she was a girl. "She looks so much like dear Eallien," they whispered, staring at me.

"How is the dog taking it?" asked Larry, a vice-principal at my father's school, and I felt my composure begin to disintegrate. After a moment I managed to say through stiff lips: "The dog died a year ago Christmas," and wondered how anyone over forty could be so fucking inept.

"Psychic Reading"
by Leslie Hill

"You want a reading? Thirty bucks. Come in here." She pointed to a sagging armchair in a cluttered living room, then sat down across from me with a coffee table between us. I handed her the money.

"I don't need to know anything about the past or the present," I said. "Just the future, please."

"I tell you what I see, I don't do timelines." She shuffled a grubby looking deck of cards and handed it to me to cut. "Use your left hand."

She turned the first card over without a comment. Put down the second.

"Looks like you've been having a rough time lately."

When she turned over the third, she shot a glance at me. I stared fixedly at the cards, which meant nothing to me and were blurring anyway.

"You've ended a relationship lately, lost someone important to you." There was a faint question in her words.

"My husband. He died. Yes."

"When?"

"Wednesday."

"*Last Wednesday?*"

I nodded. She put down the deck of cards. "But — why are you coming to see me?"

"Because you can't say anything bad. Whatever you see can't be worse than now. I thought, if you looked forward, you'd see something better, something that would ... I don't know, help me move on."

It seemed perfectly logical to me, but she stared at me in disbelief. Finally she shook her head, picked up the cards again, and started laying them out and talking fast.

"You're going to have a hard time for quite a while. Work is difficult. I see minor health problems that you might have to deal with long term. Not everyone around you is as supportive as they appear. Someone is going to demand a lot of you that you can't give and that person will be very angry with you. Money will be okay eventually but you will feel a lot of financial pressure in the short run. You'll be doing some travelling but it won't make much difference to the way you feel for a few years. Christ. Look, give me your right hand."

She had changed tactics so quickly that it took me a moment but I flattened my hand in hers. She stared grimly at the lines in my palm and then relaxed. "Okay, here's some good news; you're going to live to be over ninety."

I burst into tears.

If a narrative's predicament is likely to evoke initial discomfort or resistance in the reader within the first few pages, it is crucial to take this resistance into account and reassure your reader that he is in good hands. There are countless ways to do this. The narrator, or a character, may embody this ambivalence while at the same time conveying her need not to turn away from the narrative's unfolding. The use of well-timed humour or conflicting perspectives can assure the reader that your narrative has been well considered. Pacing of the narrative is another manner by which to signal that the narrative will not be in the reader's face — that the narrative itself understands the circuitous nature of storytelling, whether it is a poem or a novel. Pacing also acknowledges our human need for time to absorb and reflect. Curiously, narratives that provoke initial resistance often are the ones that have the greatest impact on us. They are the ones that become some of our most beloved narratives. If we do not take the reader's resistance into account, however, we then fail to effectively locate our reader, and the book will be closed within the first few minutes.

As writers, we must create the conditions to locate the reader effectively, draw her into the narrative's unique world with its own particular state of consciousness. When this happens, the reader is quickly able to make deductions and to draw inferences, much as we do in lived experience. Our tendency to write unnecessary and intrusive commentary — which I call "billboarding" — is quelled. It is not unusual, however, for writers to be unclear about what the narrative's predicament is until we are well into the first or subsequent drafts. Once we do recognize it, we must return to the opening of the narrative and revise it to accurately cue the reader.

As an exercise, you may find it useful to pull a number of books off the shelf and read only the first page of each. Which first pages excite and intrigue you most? Which ones make you eager to continue reading? Once you have found a number of such first pages, determine how each author drew you in. Which strategies used by these authors appeal to you most, give you ideas for the first page of your own narrative?

One of the most remarkable locating sentences that I have encountered is in the opening of Jamaica Kincaid's novel *The Autobiography of My Mother*: "My mother died at the moment I was born, so for my whole life there was nothing standing between myself and eternity, at my back was always a bleak, black wind."[1]

II.

Memory is our material — private or public, observed or researched, imagined or factual. All prose narratives, whether fiction or creative non-fiction, are constituted or reconfigured from various fragments of memory; narrative strategies used in fiction and creative non-fiction, however, are dissimilar. Identifying how these different prose narratives are built helps us to locate the reader effectively in each of these genres.

When writing fiction, we typically begin with a relatively small set of specific narrative elements: characters, settings, time frames, gestures, physical appearances, and possible themes. Perhaps we even have a sense of the plot. Our task is to flesh out these narrative elements and determine the story's structure. We seek to replicate, as close to the bone as possible, lived experience. Even when writing speculative fiction, lived experience must be evoked enough for the narrative's elements to be believable. When writing fiction, we gradually discover a strange familiarity with aspects of the story that we had not anticipated or imagined. We experience a knowing

---

Jamaica Kincaid, *The Autobiography of My Mother* (New York: Farrar Straus Girous, 1994).

that we cannot logically explain. If you imagine a funnel, we begin writing at the small opening and finish at the wide opening.

a handful of
fictive elements reads like creative
non-fiction

A good piece of fiction reads as realistically as creative non-fiction.

In creative non-fiction, the narrator has the narrative within her possession, and it is seemingly a matter of retelling the story. In contrast to fiction, creative non-fiction begins with an overwhelming array of memories, observations, documents, research, and, not infrequently, a cast of thousands. The central challenge with creative non-fiction is to determine the focus, select, then evoke. When writing creative non-fiction, we gradually discover aspects of the story that we had no clue about. These discoveries may arise from our research, from a new perspective gained in the reconfiguring of our material, or from our recognition of the unconscious forces that drive us to write the narrative. Using these new discoveries to guide us in determining the text's structure and focus is the key. In turn, we must offer the reader a similar discovery process, using subtle devices of déjà vu, premonition, and foreshadowing. We utilize devices of fiction to bring vivacity to the non-fiction narrative. In this sense, we begin writing at the wide opening of the funnel and end with a coherence symbolized by the small opening at the opposite end.

breathing

an array of creative non-fiction elements reads like fiction

A good creative non-fiction narrative reads as compellingly as fiction.

Reading is full of consequence.

Reading is an irreversible act of trust.

Since I began writing in the 1970s, the necessity I perceive for me and for other writers to locate the reader has increased. Diversification of communities, the migratory nature of contemporary lives, and changes in representation of reality by information technology make truth more complex, even illusive. In our first few lines, we must create the conditions for the previously assumed "handshake" between writer and reader; we must affirm that reading is an act of respect.

The Page

How can I make the page less intimidating?

The page (paper) was invented by Cai Lun during the Han Dynasty in 200 BC.

Taking his inspiration from rural people who noticed how floating catkins coagulated on the surface of water — forming a thin sheet — Cai Lun used bamboo, hemp, and silk fibres to create a rough paper. Ls'ai Tun (AD 105) improved on this papermaking process and paper quality by using the inner bark of mulberry trees and bamboo fibre.

Like paper's predecessors — cave wall, stone or clay tablet, and papyrus — the page (as we know it) embodies its own history of coming into existence: particular trees from a specific landscape, recycled paper, cloth and other organic matter, water source, heat, bleach, machines, trucks, and workers' hands. The handshake between paper and hand, hand and page, is a narrative covenant. Similar to paper, writers embody our own histories of existence: genes, familial narrative, personality, culture, race, and socio-political contexts — our life stories.

Between the page and the writer is magnetism more compelling than any other relationship.

The page is an energy field that humbles, intrigues, elates, terrifies. The page can hold any shape, embody any depth, is limited only by our hesitancies and incomprehension: our stone-carved habits of perception and inscription.

The page holds all possibilities.

breathing

Early seafaring peoples of European ancestry were afraid of falling off the edge of the world. Each time we sit down at our desks and set out to write, we are afraid of falling into the bottomlessness of the page. Is this why we pretend the page is empty?

Pag-, Latin, pagina, pagent — portable platform on which mystery plays were presented. From the three-dimensional medieval platform of pageantry and magic to our contemporary times, the page has changed into a grid into which many writers systematically insert their lines. The mystery of what passes between writer and reader when we inscribe the narrative (when it begins to take form), then compose it (when it matures into independent existence), is often considered secondary. The haste and routine of pigeonholed lines of poetry and prose compromise the power of the narrative.

The etymology of the page indicates that *pag-, pagian* refers to a "trellis to which a row of vines is fixed, hence a column of writing." Words will be words as vines will be vines, *vine, vineus, wine*, but the quality of the fruit — and end result, wine — depends on us.

The page provides a basic structural environment for words that, without it, run wild in our mind or wither from lack of space in the inhospitable soil of the spoken world. *Pag-, pagina, pail.*

Page holds anything: one moment fire, next moment water.

As the writer's subject takes shape, the smooth skin of the page soaks up some words, repels others. If we are alert, this is when the paper cuts — wakes us up. When we rub the page the wrong way, it stops responding, as do our readers. These pages are skimmed, turned, ignored. The page longs to be fully sensed — as a lover's body. Imaginatively occupied. Touched where it desires to be touched. Revered where it wishes suspension. As with a lover, routine and habit dissipate the page's power. Spontaneous mutuality is its joy.

Page is pure entrustment.

In-fluencies # 1

Fourteen stories high in the Hilton. Looking down on the Detroit River (Windsor, Ontario side). Oscar there launching the book she edited. *Silences*. Thirty-six academics writing on. The river surprisingly beautiful. Changing colours constantly with cloud shadow; the coming and going of light. Boats of all sizes plying its waters periodically at variable speeds; at various tasks. River a kind of horizon.

At sixteen years of age, Oscar made her first visit here, on the other side. The Luther League Convention. A group from her church taking the train to attend. Detroit. Their anxious mothers sewing them all matching plaid jackets: membership flags of their rural Iowa community worn on their torsos. Oscar now gazes across at Cobo Hall: site of their convention. Recalls. Viscerally. Keynote speech by Black anti-racist activist on how deeply ingrained racism is in the English language: "little white lies" contrasted to "a black lie;" "Angel Food Cake" contrasted to "Devil's Food Cake." A long list. Oscar elated by his intelligence; integrity. His exposure of English's unacknowledged biases pivotal. Language could encounter silence — pry open its sealed lips.

It was then she became a writer.

Oscar was not yet then, but only Betsy. It takes four and a half decades. In her sixtieth year, she chooses a parallel given name. Oscar. Names her unnamed self.

Oscar of Between, by Betsy Warland, a manuscript-in-progress, 2010.

Memory as Metaphor

How can I be confident about working with memories that do not coincide with those who shared them?

Everything is memory.

If you were to look around and scan the space you are currently in, could you locate anything with which you have no associative memory? You might say, "That odd outlet on the adjacent wall." You don't know what it is used for. Or the man sitting ahead of you on the bus wearing a baseball cap with two immature eagle feathers sticking out the back — you've never seen a guy quite like that before. But the fact that you can identify an electrical outlet is an act of memory, as is the fact that you can say "man," "baseball cap," and "two immature eagle feathers."

If we encounter something that is truly without memory, we either feel afraid or we fail to see it. Canoeing alone in a northern Ontario lake, I once came upon a bizarre-looking object afloat in the water. It looked like the shoulder of a prehistoric animal. Initially, I was totally unnerved. Curiosity prevailed, however, and I poked at it with my paddle and discovered it was some kind of botanical water life. Yet, with no context (memory), I didn't know if it was dangerous or harmless and I quickly paddled away.

Everything is narrative.

Narrative can only be understood through other narratives. Although each of us brings our own plethora of narratives to a "new" narrative we encounter, if it were an entirely new narrative in every respect, we would neither be able to write it nor be able to make sense of it as readers. Think of narrative as a triangle with the reader's pre-existing narratives forming one side, the writer's pre-existing narratives forming the other side, and the narrative the writer creates forming the base of the triangle. There must be enough correspondences among all three of these for a writer's narrative to circulate in a meaningful way. All three must collaborate with one another.

An example of what happens when this breaks down can be found in Gertrude Stein's writing. Despite Stein's genius, most readers (including most writers) have difficulty making sense of her writing. E.M. Forster suggests, in his book *Aspects of the Novel*, that the two central aspects of a novel are time and value; Stein's books were not more successful because most of her narratives were written independent of time. Without the referents of time, most of us lose our contextual bearings, and meaning begins to unhinge. If we return to the image of the triangle, it's as if the base of the triangle (the new narrative written by the writer) falls open, and the collaboration between the writer and the reader becomes discontinuous.

All narratives build on other narratives.

Aristotle's definition of narrative being comprised of a beginning, a middle, and an end continues to be our dominant narrative template. "Is a blade of grass a narrative?" I cannot be certain that it is, but I suspect it is familiar with narrative. A grass seed becoming a plant becoming a winter-dead blade may indeed enact this definition of narrative. Just as narratives build on narratives, blades depend on previous blades. Narrative appears to be imprinted on our souls and in every fibre of ourselves. How else can we explain a bird raised in captivity since birth — having never heard its particular species' song — still knows how to sing it?

Our material is our memory.

Even when we invent, we use composite bits of memory from lived experience and from others' experiences that we have absorbed. Western society's concept of memory is predominantly that of it being quantifiable, factual, provable, rote. In fact, memory is far more fluid, intuitive, symbolic, associative, embodied, and codified. It is invested in and forms and alters the cells of our bodies. It is by its very nature metaphoric. In Patricia Hampl's insightful essay "Memory and Imagination," she writes: "We find, in our details and broken, obscured images, the language of symbol. Here memory impulsively reaches out and embraces imagination. That is the resort to invention. It isn't a lie, but an act of necessity, as the innate urge to locate truth always is."[2]

Our body, our archive.

Scientific experiments reveal that we can focus on only 10 percent of the stimulation within and around us at any given moment. This extreme selectivity requires our memory to function in a metaphoric manner. A recent study has illuminated that we remember far more than we are conscious of remembering. Individuals were asked to enter a room and look around and exit. They

---

2.   Patricia Hampl, *I Could Tell You Stories* (New York and London: W.W. Norton & Company, 1999).

were then asked to list everything they noticed (remembered) from the room. Then they were hypnotized and asked again to write down everything they had noticed. This time they remembered two to three times more. For example, although they did not remember a newspaper in their first list, while under hypnosis they not only remembered it but also recalled the name and date of the newspaper. If we juxtapose this research with another study that determined that 90 percent of our communication with one another happens non-verbally, we realize just how formidable and fascinating our task is when we work with the materials of memory and language to construct narrative.

The concept of universality has led us to believe that art is hallmarked by its universal resonance and appeal. Universality has influenced our belief that only one version can be the true version, the true story. Multiple points of view are regarded with suspicion at best. I call this mono vision "the authorized version." It authorizes, in turn, which narratives are and are not allowed. The authorized version often prevents non-authorized narratives from even being written.

While minoring in history at university, I was taken aback when I realized that the factual account of the Second World War in North American history books is not the only authorized version. Fact-based, historical accounts of the war were published in Germany, Japan, Russia, France, Italy, England, The Netherlands, Poland — each has their own authorized version. What has circulated and been taught as historical fact in North America is only one of numerous diverse, even contradictory, authoritative accounts — yet each of these historical, non-fiction narratives still assumes a singular authority.

To understand the concept of the authorized version, we need to consider our family's relationship to the authorized family story presented to our extended family and the communities we are involved in. Typically, one person is the editor and shaper of the authorized version about the family and each of its members. Most often this is a parent. Sometimes it is another relative, such as a grandparent. The authorized version about the family is emphatically maintained. When a different version is suggested (god forbid it's suggested by an in-law!), this alternate version is belittled, ignored, or rejected through arguments, punishing silences, verbal (and even physical) attacks, and feuds lasting for decades.

The authorized version is a functional necessity.

It binds people together; it short-circuits debate so that we can function on a daily basis in a practical manner. As writers, however, we cannot afford to bypass questioning the impact the authorized version has on our writing, for it dulls and limits a fiction writer as much as it does a memoirist or poet. It is a kind of narrative death: it necessitates thoughtless inaccuracies, tedious stereotypes, unexamined lies. Particularly when working with autobiographical material, it is our desire to discover — to understand what we have not yet understood — that drives us to write. It is these very revelations and renovations that give the narrative its vitality and virtue.

A glimpse of the range of possible perspectives is illustrated in what I have come to call "the scene of the accident." Imagine there is an automobile collision at a busy city intersection. Everyone near the intersection will agree that an accident just happened. Even those looking in another direction will have heard it, assuming they are not deaf. Agreement soon changes to disparity when each person is asked, "What happened?" These conflicting accounts are engendered by literally different points of view. Further amplifying these different accounts is the fact that everyone arrives at the scene with their own related experiences already in place: different "memory banks" upon which they draw. As writers, it is crucial to keep in mind this notion of the scene of the accident in order to render points of view and perception with integrity, accuracy, transparency.

The same cup is not the same cup.

Unless there are shared or similar contexts, the particularities of lived experience will not be universally understood by our readers. Even when we think it safe to assume that we are sharing the same narrative, we are not. If I were to hold up my cup or mug in a café and ask those sitting around me to describe the mug *exactly as they each see it*, some descriptions would include a handle. Others would not (because they cannot see the handle). Some would focus on the pattern on the side, and some would perhaps describe a glimpse of the interior of the mug — as I'm holding it slightly tipped — while others might glimpse the mug's bottom as I tip it forward.

Although there are collective narratives, more of our narratives are personal, or a blend of personal and collective. We tend to be most alert and anxious about point of view when writing autobiographically based (evident to the reader that the narrative is based on personal experience) or autobiographically generated (the source of the narrative is not particularly evident) narratives, or narratives about people we know. Most writers, when working with such narratives, are keenly aware of their potential to elicit hurt and anger in those who shared the experience. As we have seen above, we not only see and remember things differently, but we render them differently from one another. It is always a risk to transform the private and the intimate into the public.

As writers, we know that our perspectives are limited. We can, however, write with conviction and eloquence when we realize that we write from one corner of any given narrative intersection; it is not possible to see the entire picture. Truth is, at best, complex, faceted, partial. With the passage of time, we can alter the previous versions of our memories within ourselves. The knowledge that truth can never be fully known is liberating; it has freed many writers to write some of their most arresting, resonant narratives.

As readers, however, we can be seduced by the notion of a true story (confession, gossip), by the sweep of the omnipotent voice. With this in mind, I usually encourage writers to "cue the reader" that their narratives are not the whole story. If you are working with characters or different persons, you can easily do this through evoking their different, even opposing, perceptions. With my poetry and prose narrative *The Bat Had Blue Eyes*, I first learned about writing from the scene of the accident, about how to indicate that the central personages sharing the same story had either forgotten it, had little memory of it, or had died: they could neither corroborate nor dispute my own narrative. I quietly cued the reader that this was not, nor could it ever be, the whole story.

Quote-tidian # 1

In order to represent the nonverbal elements of this dialogue as well as the interventions of crafting, the interviewer has included tape recorder time codes (e.g., [2-14:27]) and indicated areas that were deleted in this dialogue.

Betsy: [2-11:41] I remember having a conversation with Lee Maracle a few years ago {edit} about writing and family. She briefly talked about how many people had died in her family because life expectancy is still so much lower for First Nations people. And it struck me how I had come from a northern European lineage, and what I experience far more is my family forgetting itself — that death came more through a process of senility, dispersion, [and] Alzheimer's. [2-13:40] We spend a fair amount of time trying to forget who we are. {edit} It's very common among people of northern European descent to not talk about deeper things, to forget or reformulate our stories — to maintain control.

Aileen: Yes ...

Betsy: [2-14:27] I see this form of writing as {edit} a resistance to forgetting who we are, an attempt to be more responsible for our lives.

(I nod in agreement.)

\<Pause\>

(Cars whoosh past.)

Betsy: [2-22:23] {edit} I also want to speak about scored space.

(A car engine revs on the street.)

Betsy (cont'd): When we are working in poetry, the poem typically occupies half the page, and the rest is dead space. This is something that comes from my lived experience as a child and how I felt that the taboo, the unknown, the censored, the denied, were very powerful forms of communication. This will always be with me — this signature of my style. And it's something I'm always taking into account and something I am interested in. It is about looking at the page as an ecological system.

<Pause>

Aileen: [2-23:44] Can you elaborate?

Betsy: [2-23:50] Within ecology, we get into trouble when we only think about, for example —

Aileen: [2-24:13] We take systems out of context.

Betsy: [2-24:18] Yes, and we don't look at the impact of what we introduce into an environment, whereas an ecological sensibility has to take everything into account. In that sense, working with the scored space takes everything into account on the page. It's all alive. Everything has a necessity of being there.

(In the distance, a mother chastises her child.)

<Pause>

Aileen: {edit} [2-27:29] Yes, and connecting back to our conversation about lying: {edit} I think this is a way of giving space on the page to be present.

Betsy: [2-28:30] How I understand the "no place to hide" comment made about your writing is that the reader or listener becomes aware of their own feelings about the narrative. It's not that there is no place to hide from this overwhelming narrative — there is no place to hide from your own response to it.

"Lying: A Play in Two Acts: An interview with poet and creative non-fiction writer Betsy Warland," with Aileen Penner, *Women & Environments*, Fall/Winter 2006.

Heartwood

How can I determine what the impetus behind this narrative is?

Heartwood is the narrative's original germinating seed. It is the source from which the narrative authentically and inevitably materializes as the core of a tree's rings of growth. As a writer, you need to know what the heartwood is in each narrative to ensure that your writing finds its authentic, vital expression. Heartwood can seem so elusive that I still hesitate to even write about it.

Heartwood lingers inside the narrative surface.

At some time during inscription or composition, you may find yourself inundated with tormenting questions about why your narrative is not realizing its full power. At this point, it is crucial to identify precisely what the heartwood is in your narrative. Typically, these questions are: What writing is still to be done? What substantial revisions and deletions must be made? Why am I writing this narrative?

Heartwood is the elusive secret we keep from ourselves.

Strange as this may seem, it is not so unusual: it is your search for and discovery of heartwood that impels your writing. Heartwood most often reveals that the narrative is not quite about what you thought it was about. Sometimes you consciously realize this, sometimes you subconsciously intuit it: too often, you miss it and your narrative flounders. When you have recognized the heartwood seed of your narrative, most frustration and doubt cease as your confidence in rendering the narrative and the narrative's imperative grow together. The heartwood informs and guides you, giving you a solid basis upon which to address questions of composition.

Heartwood locates us in the seed and then the sap of experience.

To enable you to identify what heartwood is, you might consider what heartwood isn't. Heartwood isn't the prose or poetry's theme, or premise, or an encapsulation of the narrative. These are secondary and conceptual explanations — they provoke discussion, debate, analysis, summation. Theses are based on them, back cover book blurbs are written about them. They depend upon an interpretive distance.

Heartwood is profoundly, even shockingly, intimate.

E.M. Forster, writing about characters and situations in his book *Aspects of the Novel*, might as well be writing about the generative, symbolic power of heartwood when he writes: "My theory being that the actual event practically does not exist — nor time either ... they always stand for more than themselves; infinity attends them...."[1] Heartwood does not explain a seminal event. Heartwood locates us in the moment of inception; and the narrative's concentric circles swell out from its centre.

Technically, heartwood is the matrix for all other tissue. It is the central, now inactive original wood of a sapling. Sometimes it is called deadwood. Sapwood is the more newly formed outer wood that holds the sap and water and nutrient life of the tree. This may

---

1. E.M. Forster, *Aspects of the Novel* (New York: Harcourt, Brace and Company, 1927).

be why a narrative's heartwood does not hold as much power for the reader as for the writer. The seed may never be apparent to the reader, who is interested only in the tree.

Our relationship to heartwood is not time-bound. Although the seed is technically dead, in the writer it remains very much alive. Our urgency as writers, then, is to ensure that the force of that seed lives out its narrative consequences in our readers. In this way we place the reader on the growing edge of the narrative's uncertainties.

One poet I worked with identified her manuscript's heartwood as "[she] avoids her own goodness." A novelist who had been writing her novel for four years was stunned by heartwood one day when a single word suddenly floated above her manuscript. Another writer acknowledged that the process of identifying his heartwood sentence in his narrative "flattened me. After all this time of NOT writing about MY family — having invented characters, obsessions, situations, I realized that it really is about a family — who lies about everything — which is my family — on a good day." This writer may shift his narrative to a more apparent, autobiographical text, but he is as likely not to do so. The knowledge of his narrative's heartwood will, however, bring sharper focus and intensity to his fictional characters and situations now that he knows what generates his narrative.

It can take many attempts, even years, to find the heartwood of a narrative. In truth, heartwood only reveals itself when we are ready to recognize and respect it. In this manuscript, which took twelve years to write, it was only in the last year and a half that I could finally identify what was holding it all together: every essay investigates what the writer's specific state of consciousness and proximity is to each narrative she writes, and the materials with which she writes it. When our preconceived ideas about a narrative, unexamined habits of inscription, and inattentiveness to the materials with which we write render inaccurate proximity, our narrative's state of consciousness becomes askew.

It is useful to look for heartwood from time to time in a narrative we are writing, whether it is a poem or a chapter book, as this teaches us how to recognize what heartwood isn't, which later helps us recognize what it is. It can't be forced, however: this only results in error and frustration. We need to search with curiosity: abandon our preconceptions of what we believe our narrative is about; dispense with our normal ways of reading and assessing our prose or poems, using our right-brain perceptual modes; and accept that it usually requires periodic attempts before we find it. Heartwood possesses a simple yet intensely generative quality. For me, it is luminous.

I believe every narrative knows where it is going; it knows what it is about. As its writer, we also sense this, but are often unable to articulate what it is about beyond obvious, rather superficial terms. Our inability to articulate heartwood is what urges us to write. When, however, we are moving from the inscription stage (getting it down) to the composing stage (revision), our recognition of heartwood is crucial as it guides us accurately in all aspects of our revisions.

The Pencil

Why would I use a pencil when writing in longhand?

There is a deep familiarity between pencil and hand.

Our bodies fit perfectly. The pencil's hexagon shape responds immediately to the embrace of my fingers. Always we are eager for one another, to make something new each time we touch. The pencil's scent never fails to arouse. For long hours we follow trails of a thought, momentum of a narrative, surprise of a poem, intrigue of words.

We mark. We pause. We erase.

We mark. We erase. We pause.

Sharpen.

Within these pauses are other intimacies: the pencil tucked into the privacy behind our ear; the fragrance of the pencil while being sharpened; the pencil welcomed by our parting lips and teeth. Sometimes the teeth push through yellow-thin skin to savoury wood: it is we who leave marks.

A relatively recent invention, the pencil has become so integral to our everyday lives as to be overlooked in most encyclopedias and books documenting the histories of inventions. Jacques-Nicolas Conté developed the pencil during the first half of the sixteenth century in France. Inspired by the necessities of his dual professions of illustrator (art) and biologist (science), the pencil consisted of carbon (necessary to life and present in more than one million chemical compounds) and cedar (the sacred tree of many ancient societies).

Art and science. Cedar and carbon. Sacred and secular.

The interplay of the pencil: the pencil requires the right play between hand, point, page, and our writing surface. Just like conversation must be taut yet flowing. If we press too hard, its point snaps — like a tense word breaks our trust.

Pencil, Latin, penicillus, brush, diminutive of penis, "*small tail.*" Like the tail movement of the dog, cat, and wolf, pencil marks signal one another on the page.

The pencil embodies the temporality of narrative (which must be endlessly renewed or re-formed), for with usage we watch the pencil decrease. A pencil on average writes 45,000 words. It signals time's passage, urging us on to the next word, the next page. Our hand intimately knows a particular, curious, accumulating sadness as pencil becomes smaller, smaller, until it is too small to hold. Reluctantly, we throw pencil stub away. Wonder what its final two inches might have enabled us to write.

With the 180 degrees back and forth turning of the pencil, we inscribe and obliterate, create and destroy. Alpha and Omega. Pencil embodies the interdependent relationship of existence as not opposites but crests and troughs of being, of knowing and forgetting.

Embodiment

My narratives tend to veer off or lose momentum. How can I maintain focus effectively?

The body is far wiser about narrative than consciousness will ever be.

All the formal and narrative elements of poetry and prose originate in our bodies. Like the heart, our sense of time expands and contracts. An initial walk to a writing hut in the forest seems three times longer in contrast to our return along the now more familiar path.

Time expands. Contracts. So does the narrative line.

A luminous moment can contain years of lived experience. Inside the dialogue of cells and organs, we read the plots of our growing and aging bodies. The paired iambic pentameter of our brain hemispheres, eyes, ears, nostrils, arms, lungs, hands, kidneys, legs, and feet collaboratively maintain the underlying rhythm with which writing is shaped. Daphne Marlatt writes, "the beginning: language, a living body we enter at birth, sustains and contains us."[1]

Compelling writing emits from embodiment: provokes embodiment in the reader. Typically, we tend to think that certain subjects and forms include, or exclude, embodiment. Why is this so? Is it because we see body as boundary endlessly attempting to defend itself against the intrusiveness of life around us, while — at the same time — it obsessively longs for submersion, satiety? Could our

---

1. Daphne Marlatt, *Touch to My Tongue* (Edmonton: Longspoon Press, 1984).

breathing

revering of universality in art be a kind of nostalgic reminiscence of being *in utero*?

Most of us would agree that writing that has the greatest impact invariably draws upon the logic, mystery, and metaphoric nature of the entire body. It is writing that is not composed from the shoulders up. Learning how to focus is one of our biggest challenges as writers. We get a rare glimpse of total, preparatory focus when a basketball player pauses and readies himself at the free throw line, or when a golfer determines her strategy and gathers her concentration before making a putt, or when a diver internally organizes her whole body before springing off the high diving board.

As writers, we must learn how to navigate through three preparatory stages of focus every time we sit down to inscribe a first draft. First is the stage during which we accumulate our thoughts, images, intuitions, research, and notes. This is the circling stage. In *open is broken* (1984), I describe it by way of etymology:

MARK: merg — boundary, border, marking out the boundary by walking around it (ceremonially "beating the bounds").

This initial stage can take a few hours up to a few years, depending on the scope of the writing project, the time we have available to circle, and how well we manage to stay on the narrative's scent, as in "When the pen gets on the scent" (Virginia Woolf, *A Writer's Diary*).[2]

---

2. Virginia Woolf, *A Writer's Diary* (Frogmore, St. Albans: Triad/Panther Books, 1979).

The second preparatory focus stage is the approach, or, as we might call it, "crossing the threshold." This stage may appear to be rather insignificant, but it is, in fact, pivotal. During this preparatory stage we engage in some kind of activity that transports us away from the demands, interruptions, assumptions, and distractions of our daily life into our nascent narrative's particular state of consciousness. For me, activities involving motion and no language (walking, biking, travelling on a boat, bus, or train) work well. Sitting quietly with a cup of tea or performing a simple physical task that requires neither thought nor conversation also suits.

The third stage is the active waiting stage as we sit at our writing site. This focus stage is most akin to the basketball player gathering his focus at the free throw line. I find that many writers are reluctant to trust this preparatory focus stage (which is not to be confused with procrastination). I often remain in this final preparatory stage of active waiting for considerable lengths of time as I wait for the narrative to reveal its true opening to me. When pressured by time — as we writers frequently are — we can easily become anxious to write. We can mistake speed of inscription for inspiration. This is how we become susceptible to rushing down many false paths that lead us away from what our narrative requires, and our narrative gets off track — sometimes for pages and pages — even chapters. Authentic narrative path openings, however, possess a distinct quality of radiance, rawness, surprising rupture or synchronicity, even remorselessness. In her book *If You Want To Write*, Brenda Ueland describes how she used coffee and cigarettes to jump-start inspiration and productivity. Over time, she became aware of a dissatisfaction with the quality of her writing and gradually replaced coffee and cigarettes with a long morning walk. It was during these walks that she discovered the benefits of what she affectionately named "moodling." This was when her writing began to improve notably.[3]

The heartwood seed of some narratives can seem to fall out of the sky — perfectly formed — into our laps: these are gifts, and these are rare. From observing myself and many other writers I know, most narratives circle us countless times (when we are attempting to circle them!) until they are certain of inviting us in. Like Emily Dickinson's "telling it at a slant," or H.D.'s waking visions of words on the wall, a genuine narrative allows itself to be observed only in elliptical glimpses from the corner of our eye.

During our inscription process it is crucial to be fully present to the narrative (and its inherent form) just as it is essential to be present in any intimate relationship. If we are ambiguous or impatient, the narrative will respond accordingly. Kristjana Gunnars's challenge to writers in her book *Stranger at the Door: Writers and the Act of Writing* is one that we must always meet: "If you are not able to function inside the uncertainties, and doubts and absences the writing act will engage you in, you are lost before you begin."[4]

If I can state anything with certainty after writing for forty-five years and teaching for twenty-five, it is this: we cannot fool the narrative. And, equally important, our prevaricating narrative will not fool an astute reader: our reader will become disinterested, distrustful, irritated.

---

3. Brenda Ueland, *If You Want to Write* (Saint Paul: Graywolf Press, 1987).
4. Kristjana Gunnars, *Stranger at the Door: Writers and the Act of Writing* (Waterloo: Wilfrid Laurier University Press, 2004).

It is almost impossible to evoke the non-verbal too much — this is another indicator of how crucial embodiment is. It is always humbling for us to remember that research has confirmed that up to 90 percent of how we communicate is non-verbal. This is one reason reading your work into a tape recorder can open up other forms of perception such as intonation, implication, gesture. One poet who did this described her experience to me: "I ended up reading the whole manuscript into the tape recorder and then I listened to it in complete darkness a few days later. This helped me to tap an area of the brain that I hadn't before and helped me to identify natural connections between poems as well as some gaps in the narrative."[5]

Deep listening takes time. Lots of it. When deaf people are able to gain a significant amount of hearing through hearing aids or cochlear implants, they must concentrate far more on listening than on producing language. To an "untrained" ear, language is a cacophony, or a blur of sounds. Words are not perceived as separate things, units of meaning, having innate relevance. Each word must be laboriously isolated, identified, and repeated again and again until it is integrated. Then the deaf person must learn to select, order, and articulate accurately each word to communicate successfully with others. With writing, it is much the same.

Throughout the inscription process it is wise to remind ourselves about the benefits of working orally. As a poet, it is absolutely essential to sound out your poem over and over throughout the inscription, composition, and revision processes. In prose, this

---

5.   Astrid van der Pol, about her book *Invisible Lines* (Ottawa: Buschekbooks, 2003).

breathing

sounding out is also vital to writing authentic dialogue. Tone, transitions, indicative pauses, distinction of characters' voices, pace — all can be assessed more accurately through listening. This is how we develop our third ear. It's as if your entire body becomes a third ear, freed from the listening habits of our actual ears. Keep in mind that reading your work "aloud" in your mind does not activate your third ear. To access your third ear it is necessary to read your work out loud, ask a skillful reader to read your work aloud while you listen, or read your work into a tape recorder. As you do this, make every effort to allow the writing to read itself: refrain from imposing how you think it should sound. These methods allow you to focus your complete attention on hearing where the writing moves effectively and effortlessly and where it fails to do so.

Ultimately, we can't beat a live audience. I believe that poets and prose writers alike need to read their work to an audience prior to publication. It is here, in this 3-D auditory environment, that our third ear is fully activated. Spots where the narrative still is in need of revision become remarkably obvious.

Routinely scanning or "reading" our bodies throughout our inscription, composition, and revision process is another method of anchoring ourselves in embodiment and the narrative's corresponding state of consciousness. Our body often possesses the information and guidance that we need in sensing what each narrative requires.

Scan the "body of your text" using your own body's radar to note repetition of line structure (order, rhythm, sounds) and repetition of words and images. Sometimes unintentional repetition is attempting to flag you — alert you to a place in the narrative that requires more "unpacking" or lingering.

Although unintended repetition is often a powerful key to unconscious intentions, as often it is a habit of inscription. It is well worth it to take the time to identify exactly what your habits of repetition are: recurring words; opening phrases of lines; line, stanza, and paragraph structure. Only then can you distinguish between forms of repetition that you need to avoid and forms of repetition that are attempting to flag your attention to areas in the narrative that are not resolved.

Habits of repetition we are extremely resistant to changing are the very ones we need to explore and change. They often contain important insights about our inscription process that routinely limit and dull our narratives — do we repeatedly use the same sentence structure regardless of the sentence content? We can, with increased awareness, also learn how to use our habits choice-fully and effectively, to make them signatures of our style (one for me is using the article *the* sparingly in lyric prose and poetry).

Let's return to this essay's opening sentence: "The body is far wiser about narrative than consciousness will ever be." I maintain that the narrative not only knows where it is going but also knows what it is about, whether it is an occasional poem or a creative non-fiction book. As writers, our challenge is to learn how to follow each narrative's requirements, each narrative's particular state of consciousness: this is when we trust its quirky logic; this is when it makes absolute sense to our reader; this is when our difficulties with determining and maintaining focus disappear. Frank Bidart, commenting on Coleridge's concept of organic form, notes that "form must embody what is already there."[6]

One author I worked with was plagued by sleepiness when she wrote. She had not had this problem before. There seemed to be no logical explanation. We investigated when her sleepiness tended to occur during her inscription process and what she was writing about when sleepiness overtook her. A pattern began to emerge gesturing to an underlying narrative. She had dismissed this underlying narrative as too painful. She was ambivalent about including it, but the narrative required it. Once she accepted this, her sleepiness disappeared.

When we become fully embodied in the visceral environment from which our narrative emerges, then our narrative is fully embodied. In his book of essays, *Body Music*, Dennis Lee writes: "The most common single voice in contemporary poetry is the one which *states* 'I think of how you betrayed me, and I feel angry.'"

What does that voice embody? A discursive equanimity, which reports on its feelings (and everything else) with arm's-length detachment ... The poem no more "feels angry" than it feels pink.[7]

We write incrementally during inscription, composition, and revision, and from time to time we must also assess the narrative incrementally. Accessing information and insight via our own embodiment in each narrative is one of our most reliable sources.

---

6. Frank Bidart, "Thinking through Form" in David Lehman, ed., *Ecstatic Occasions, Expedient Forms: 85 Leading Contemporary Poets Select and Comment on Their Poems* (Ann Arbor: University of Michigan Press, [1987] 1996).

7. Dennis Lee, *Body Music* (Toronto: House of Anansi Press, 1998).

Quote-tidian # 2

rob mclennan: What is the best piece of advice you've heard, not necessarily given to you directly?

Betsy Warland: I came across it a couple of decades ago in Virginia Woolf — *A Writer's Diary*: "when the pen gets on the scent." This has been my guiding mantra ever since. We can only write incrementally — one word at a time — just as a dog sniffs the trail of a specific animal or person — we must recognize each narrative's distinct scent. When we are on the scent of the narrative it is a visceral, elating, and sometimes terrifying experience. Doubt and confusion drop away. We trust where the narrative's momentum and trajectory will take us. It's not that we have it all figured out, but rather that we are wholly inside each idiosyncratic step of how that narrative goes about building itself.

"12 or 20 questions: with Betsy Warland," interview with rob mclennan, 12or20questions.blogspot.com, 18/02/08.

The Alphabet

Is the alphabet anything more than a tool?

The alphabet not only enables our written narratives, but it also embodies its own narrative.

Alphabet: alph, the first letter of the Greek alphabet, the first of anything + beta, the second letter of the Greek alphabet, the second item in a series or system.

Once there are two there are more.

Sumerian cuneiform script of the thirty-fourth century BC is believed to be the first writing, and it is a precursor to our alphabet. The origins of our phonetic alphabetic letters trace back to the Phoenicians and Semites of Syria and Palestine around 1000 BC.

ΚΚ𝕶 𐤀AAA AAA ᴧᴀ A𝑎a𝑎

| Phoenician | Greek | Roman | Medieval | Modern |

Many of these precursory letters were graphic symbols that depicted the basic forms of everyday life:

- A, alph, "ox"
- B, beth, "house"
- C and G, gimel, "camel"
- D, daleth, "door"
- I and J, yod, "hand"
- K, kaph, "hollow of the hand"
- M, mem, "water"

- N, nun, and X, smekh, "fish"
- O, cayin, "eye"
- P, pe, "mouth"
- Q, qoph, "monkey"
- R, resh, "head"
- S, shin, "tooth"
- T, taw, "mark"

Shapes of the natural world also appear: the *M* of mountain peaks; the slithering *S* of snake; the *O* of moon.

Unlike footprints involuntarily left behind, the alphabet's letters are more akin to mammals' intentionally left scents that warn, excite, guide, or invite — informing others and infusing their own memory for retracing their steps later. Letters forming words function in much the same way.

Alphabet connotes our absence.

Conceptually and instinctively, the alphabet's lineage is picto-grams, ideograms, hieroglyphs, and petroglyphs.

Like these other systems, the act of inscribing letters of alphabet embodies our own particular presence outside or beyond our physical body. Our textual bodies then circulate in a random, sensuous, unlimited manner as a note in a bottle at sea, astral travel, or seeds on feet of migrating birds.

With the advancement of civilization, the alphabet became a strategy for not getting lost: a map. Small-scale, basic survival nomadism was gradually replaced by large-scale economic, religious, and cultural "nomadism." Letters — like storage pots — contained the essences (scents) of one's origins that could be retrieved and activated by their users, passed on to their offspring and to those with whom they co-existed or traded, or those whom they conquered.

With unprecedented expansion, and the necessity to bridge our greater differences, came the realization that our human voice was no longer sufficient. The voice's range requires close proximity.

In *Break Every Rule*, Carol Maso affirms this when she sees us "huddled around the fire of the alphabet."[1] In *The Spell of the Sensuous*, David Abrams explores the intimate relationship between language and landscape — how words have the power to enhance or stifle the spontaneous life of our senses: "to read is to enter into a profound participation, or chiasm, with the inked marks on the page."[2]

When reciting the alphabet out loud, the vowels' free passage of breath opens outward — then crests periodically — between the accumulating waves of consonants' partial or complete obstruction of the air stream. The alphabet replicates our lungs' movements — breathing itself — as air animates voice, the alphabet animates page.

Breath is life.

If breath is believed to be a manifestation of the deities, vowels may be the vestiges of divine speech. An infant's early word-sounds are nearly all vowels. Our final dying word is often a vowel. It is

1. Carol Maso, *Break Every Rule* (Washington, D.C.: Counterpoint, 2000).

2. David Abrams, *The Spell of the Sensuous* (New York: Pantheon Books, 1996).

with the vowel we come into this life from elsewhere. It is with the vowel we leave this life for elsewhere. Throughout our life, *Latin*, *vowel*, *vox*, *voice* persistently seeks *consonant*, *Latin*, *consonare*, *to harmonize*.

This is the alphabet's spell.

The Coma Story and the Comma Story

When my narrative subjects are different, why do they end up sounding the same?

A coma story is an autobiographically based story that we tell and retell. Usually it is a story about a lived experience from the past that was difficult, remarkable, pivotal, or humorous. Often a coma story is an embroidered or exaggerated lived-experience story. With the repetitive telling of particular coma stories the teller soon believes them to be unquestionably true. All coma stories are told for the purpose of entrenching a perspective that the teller prefers listeners maintain about the teller, or about his story's subjects. Myths and sacred stories differ from the coma story as they are constructed with underlying levels of meanings and are concerned with maintaining a long-standing community.

How can we spot a coma story imprinting itself on our writing? Typically, coma stories use simple language and narrative structure that often include clichés and stereotyping. They are relatively short. They are told exactly the same time after time and, not infrequently, are told throughout one's lifetime. They smooth over complexities and contradictions. Although typically based on one's lived experience, coma stories can also be hand-me-down coma stories passed on to us via a family member.

I call these stories *coma stories* because their narratives are hermetically sealed. The teller and the listener are in a static, predictable relationship, for the teller will not allow any variation or disparity. When challenged, arguments will often ensue between the teller and listener(s). Although the act of forming such stories is liberating initially — making events and our perspectives evident to others — they quickly entrap us in our habitual retelling of them.

For a writer, a coma story may provide the initial impetus for a narrative. These narratives may become realized in any genre. *Bloodroot: Tracing the Untelling of Motherloss* is an example of this in my own writing process. I had a coma story about how my mother would never really want to know who I was. A year prior to her death, she confessed to me she "had another daughter" whom she wanted me to meet. My mother frequently lapsed into senility. I had learned not to correct her, but to follow her circuitous logic. This time, the other daughter turned out to be a metaphor for me — her actual daughter — the daughter she didn't know. If I had clung to my coma story, I would have never allowed this remarkable opening my mother gave me: I would have quickly corrected her error, and our relationship would have remained sadly static. I would have not recognized the gift being offered to me that later became *Bloodroot*.

When we recognize the trance we fall into, we can then awaken ourselves from the coma story's grip on our narrative. Though we tend to think of a trance in terms of hypnosis, it more frequently is a state of being dazed, a state of being detached from our physical surroundings and our bodies.

As we re-sensitize, we begin to see that there is a difference between fidelity to an event and what Denise Levertov calls "fidelity to experience." Recounting an event results in reportage — we fail to awaken from the coma. Recreating the unfolding of an event immediately locates both writer and reader inside the unpredictability and subtleties of that specific experience. This is the effect that we are after: it is the dynamic experience that we are intrigued by, not the static event. In the process of writing *only this blue*, it wasn't the specific causes of my life-threatening illness that magnetized me to write, but rather how this experience altered my encounter with ordinary daily things so dramatically that it forever changed my perception of them. This was what I found most disorienting, yet invigorating.

As a writer, it is essential that you study the narrative structure of your coma story. Why? Because your story may appear to change, but the underlying template of the original coma story still retains its hold. Our template forms the habits with which we unthinkingly and repeatedly inscribe our poetry or prose. Our templates are usually poor fits for our non-coma narratives: their forms most often are at odds with the narrative. The fit can be so inappropriate that it not only alters the writer's narrative intentions but also distorts the narrative itself. One poet with whom I worked on manuscript development had a template preventing her from discerning her true narrative. She had a tangent of poems that she kept dismissing: they didn't fit in with her concept of the real story narrative. Upon reading her manuscript, I asked to read her tangent poems and discovered that these poems possessed remarkable energy and originality. Once she extracted herself from her templates, she recognized their worth, and they became the sole basis of her new manuscript, for which eventually she received a national award.

The value in coma stories is that they are an efficient method of memory retention. When recounted, our intimates automatically fill in the blanks. Our readers, however — outside this close circle — do not. Coma stories function as a personal codification system that can, when worked with consciously, connect us to the narrative we long to access. A narrative about being a tree planter in a remote region of British Columbia can read like a coma story when written as a description of the job. Or it can take us there by evoking the philosophical, sociological, and political states of reflection prompted by work that drives you to the very precipice of your mental and physical capacities.

If we lack this larger narrative awareness, we are easily seduced by the comfort and the predictability of a coma story. This makes the narrative easier to write. All too often, however, it results in a loss of the reader's attention. As writers, we are often troubled by a dull sense of something missing. When you hear a voice saying, "The reader really doesn't want or need to know about this," you are likely in the clutches of a coma story. This is when you know it is time to surrender to the real power trapped inside the coma story: let the story tell itself. Then our narrative seizes its life.

When I encounter a coma story, I ask the writer to elaborate verbally about her narrative. Almost without fail, she begins to decode the coma, and the narrative becomes far more engaging. Upon my remarking on this, usually the response is, "It's already there" in the poem or the scene. I ask her to point this out on the page. Most writers are surprised to discover that it is not there — that it is still locked in their minds. At this exciting point, a writer can puncture her hermetically sealed poem or piece of prose by writing into the commas of a coma story. As Ezra Pound says, "Make it new." For each comma — figurative or literal — is a potential opening to what has been left out, what imaginative and associative possibilities the coma story seeks.

Most commas function as appropriate grammatical signals of pauses or separations within a fully realized sentence or lyric line: there is no need to write into them. We must, however, investigate, even interrogate, those pauses and separations, inscribed by a literal or figurative comma, that signal what the narrative requires. We might think of these commas as the currents of a river. If we write only about the water, we remain on the surface of the coma story. If we write into the currents, then the narrative pulls us along of its own free will and we do not know what will be revealed, how the narrative will move, nor how it will end.

Keep in mind that imagined — completely fictional — stories can also become coma stories. As writers, we can become fixated on our original idea for a narrative and refuse to recognize what the narrative's requirements are.

How do we consistently recognize a coma story? Some typical signals for which to look are: abrupt transitions; patches of awkward syntax; tangents; generalized, clichéd lines or phrases that camouflage complexities; images or words that unintentionally appear repeatedly; gaps; or juxtapositions of lines or sections that inexplicably don't add up.

As an exercise, write a coma story that's related, directly or indirectly, to your writing project or subject. To do this, it should be a story you have told numerous times in the same way. Make every attempt to render it exactly as you tell it — refrain from making it literary or from explaining or improving any aspect of it. After you have written this coma story, write into a comma by doing one or more of the following:

- Insert a comma before the first word of the story and write whatever comes to you into that comma.
- Insert a comma anywhere in the story where you know or

sense there's more to tell — including the censored or dismissed — and write into that comma.

- Delete the period at the end of the story and replace it with a comma and write into that open space. It may be productive to set a timer and allow yourself to do a free-writing exercise for five minutes without pausing or judging it.

When we have become proficient in knowing our coma story templates, our writing will still migrate in and out of it. It can happen from one poetic line to the next, from one paragraph to the next, from one chapter or one narrative to the next. Sometimes the coma story, although initially crucial to building a narrative, must be removed later just as a builder removes scaffolding in later stages of construction.

Occasionally, the nature of a particular narrative requires that we consciously work the edge between the coma and comma, as this is an inherent struggle within the narrative itself. The pervasive power of the coma story and its formal template can never be overestimated. When, however, we write into the surprising narrative territory of the commas, our narratives pulse on the page.

Quote-tidian # 3

Arleen Paré: I am beginning to think that so much of what you are talking about is coming from the body. What we have to work with is this body, in all these ways.

Betsy Warland: Yes.

Arleen Paré: You wrote, "Like narrative, we spend our entire life finding out about what the story is, about our compositional strategies."

Betsy Warland: I wrote that?

Arleen Paré: You did. I was very intrigued.

Betsy Warland: Ahh! It's from "Spatiotemporal Structural Strategies." It's been quite a while since I worked on that one. That sentence sounds so clunky — I've revised it since then! Yes, with narrative we spend our entire life trying to figure out what the stories are behind our signature compositional strategies.

Arleen Paré: Yeah, yeah.

Betsy Warland: Yeah. With compositional strategies (everybody has them) — we are often not aware of them, or, vaguely, we are — we do the same thing over and over again. But their nature is not to be static. When we consciously work with them, they are always presenting us with new challenges, new questions. They are not so much intellectually based, even though we talk about them as such, but based in our body. The quest is: which forms or strategies were we deeply immersed in during the early years of our life? And how can they become dynamic signatures of our style? We can form conceptual ideas about them, but only after we've been consciously working with them for a while.

Unpublished interview with Arleen Paré, 2003.

Proximity

What is making me or my reader feel distant from my narrative?

I.

Suppose that you have written a poem about an intensely traumatic encounter, but the reader experiences the poem essentially as a detached observer. Understandably, you find this response not only disappointing but also puzzling. You could blame the reader, but this is rarely where the problem lies. Often the underlying issue is what I call "errors in proximity."

A graphic metaphor I often use when discussing proximity is a burning house. Imagine the difference between a sound byte being told by a television reporter on the sidewalk and an account by the woman who almost failed to find her way out of the burning house. You can sense how different these two narratives would be. Each narrator's proximity and version — which is what is at stake — is radically different. The apparent same story is not the same story.

To experience two very different proximities in the same narrative, select an unfinished piece of prose or poetry and write two new versions, one in which the narrator is located entirely inside the narrative and the other in which the narrator is observing and commenting on the narrative action. As you read them, what do the different proximities evoke? Reveal?

One way to think about proximity is to think of it cinematically, to equate where the camera locates you in a film with where you locate the reader at any given time in your narrative. Then develop the habit of routinely asking yourself: At this point, should the camera (the reader) be in close-up, mid-range, or panorama? Does the camera jump around? Does it remain pretty much in the same position? The more precise proximity is, the more the reader notices the subtleties in all forms of relationships as they shift, unfold, and find some kind of resolution.

When we receive the feedback "tell me more," this may point to a gap in the narrative, but far more often it points to inaccurate use of proximity. It is a question of giving the right signal. The language itself may be the problem. For example, it may be too formal and distancing when the narrative's content is drawing the reader close. This double message confuses readers, places them outside the narrative by making them observers. It also distracts them. They get caught in an eddy of confusion, just as we are confused in a conversation when someone smiles warmly while using abrasive words or distancing tones.

Proximity shapes meaning. Imagine someone saying to you "I am here," in these two different proximities: leaning down and whispering it in your ear; shouting it from a room away. The different proximities of this identical sentence convey disparate meanings.

In the English language, this embedded distancing is in the pronouns themselves. Moving from close proximity to increasingly distant proximity, the number of letters in each pronoun increases: I, me, we, he, she, you, our, they, them, those, and (the noun) people.

II.

Another way to understand proximity is to think of viewing paintings in an art gallery. Do you maintain the same proximity to each painting? Do you mechanically advance in a straight line down each wall, stopping for the same amount of time as you look at each painting?

Typically, we draw closer to examine a detail in a painting, back away to review it in its larger context, glance across the room at another image that suddenly resonates with this one, move on to the next painting, and then, a few paintings later, return to the first painting that magnetized us to compare the artist's use of similar and dissimilar strategies, or how the artist's paintings are "in conversation" with one another.

Almost all narratives coalesce with the passage of time; they take shape incrementally, even erratically. Perception also builds incrementally, whether emotional, intellectual, or spiritual. We may think we have an utterly surprising flash of insight, but the groundwork to understand this insight was laid prior to our recognition. The very structure of perception involves a cyclical process that I call "Approach — Retreat — Return." Sometimes this cycle repeats a few times; sometimes it repeats countless times. Sometimes perception is stuck for a while in one mode: Retreat — Retreat — Retreat. The cycle depends on the nature of each narrative. It also depends on our ability, as well as our readiness, to grasp the precise nature of each narrative. The narratives that have a profound impact on readers utilize Approach — Retreat — Return, evoking the telling nuances and shifts in proximity that shape and enable perception.

III.

Inaccurate proximity occurs for a number of reasons. In a line of a poem or sentence, one word can shift the proximity: "the stubble cutting my bare feet" compared with "stubble cutting my bare feet."

Proximity problems may also occur when we overlook the underlying significance of an encounter. Let's look at an excerpt from a short story in which a writer revises her rendering of proximity for more exactitude.

"When We Sat Down to Dinner" (original draft)
by Anne Souther

When we sat down to dinner, I looked at their faces, and imagined holding my hands against their contours, my fingers framing their features like parentheses.

I imagined holding between my hands their thoughts, their fears, the hopes and dreams of each of them, so entirely private that I was overwhelmed by the intimacy of it and by reflex I put my hands to my own face, framing my cheekbones and chin.

"You all right, Connie?" Ben asked. Tony and Joey stopped chewing and watched me.

"When We Sat Down to Dinner" (revised with closer attention to proximity)

When we sit down to dinner, I look at their faces, and imagine holding my hands against their contours, my fingers framing their features like parentheses. *I imagine touching their skin, feeling the tissue and the bones underneath, feeling even the blood coursing through capillaries and veins and arteries far below the expressions of concern and confusion that I see on their faces.*

I imagine holding between my hands their thoughts, their fears, the hopes and dreams of each of them, so entirely private that I am overwhelmed by the intimacy of it, and by reflex I put my hands to my own face, framing my cheekbones and chin, *daring my own mind to seep out and be revealed.*

"You all right, Connie?" Ben asks. Tony and Joey stop chewing and watch me. *They hide behind restrained expressions, but I can see the alarm in their eyes.*

Note the change in tense from the original excerpt to the revised proximity excerpt. This change from past to present tense intensifies the scene. The writer has cued the reader more accurately to the struggle between simultaneous proximities by splicing in segments of her inner monologue.

Proximity problems may also occur when spatial relationships between content and narrator change from first person to second or third person, or vice versa. I encountered such shifting of points of view while writing *only this blue*. The narrator's proximity to her subject veers from intimate encounters with herself (first person) to observation of, and sometimes disassociation with, herself (third person) to an inclusive "you" (second person).

If a narrative is overwhelming to read; if it keeps the reader unintentionally at a distance; if the voice seems to be obscuring itself or foregrounding itself inappropriately, the narrative may be set in the wrong voice. Some narratives require intentional juxtapositions of proximities to track their unpredictable paths, actions, and insights. Note how Ingrid Rose enacts this in the excerpt from her lyric prose novel below.

"In the thick of it"
by Ingrid Rose

he edges his way out of the sofa is up
pushing his narrow feet more firmly
into his wine red slippers
shuffles over to me
his thin arms
round me a moment
quick peck on cheek
hand remains on shoulder
as if to protect
or hold me back
turns to his seat again
stepping on the paper
I spy under my lashes
my mother's back straight
eyes ahead
to the next hurdle

morris look what you're doing to that paper

the quick of her voice mettled

my father raises his foot
sweeps the sheets into an untidy heap
his nervous fingers tapping the edges
to line them up

An excellent example of using proximity seamlessly in the first page of a book is Anne Stone's novel *delible*. The opening scene on the first page is entrancing, yet disturbing. Stone conveys her confidence in the narrative (which assures our confidence) by beginning with a close-up, then moving to mid-range, then pan, then close-up, then back to mid-range, then pan within the first five sentences.

The most common reasons why we neglect to check for correct proximity are our unwillingness to allow our narrative to become more complex or our failure to remove first draft scaffolding that helped us build the narrative. To be true to the story often requires considerably more writing or revision than we had imagined — or want to undertake. But when proximity is faulty, the narrative's state of consciousness becomes derailed, and our reader rightfully loses interest. Errors in proximity occur too when we are so concerned about writing the narrative that we unthinkingly revert to our habitual methods of inscription. Or when we may be uneasy about the effect of accurate proximity. If we fear our narrative may overwhelm our readers, cause them to disengage, or make us too vulnerable, we may opt for a reductive approach.

With this book I encountered proximity questions in selecting the titles of the essays. Many of them, such as this essay's title, do not automatically signal what the essay is about. Yet, the title is accurate. Eventually I came up with the idea of a hook question placed immediately below the title, a question that addresses what the essay is about. The title is more formal and distant, but the question, which may be one that engages writers, is close-up.

When reviewing appropriate use of proximity, check the following methods of inscription:

- tone
- pacing
- use of first/second/third person
- rhythmic and structural movement of the line;
- specific language of the line; spatial/contextual relationships between the lines, paragraphs, stanzas, characters, or subjects
- correspondences between discrete yet interrelated pieces (poems in a suite, sections of an essay, sections or chapters of a book)

Throughout our inscription and composition process, it is useful to routinely ask ourselves three proximity questions:

- What is the exact proximity of the characters/people in this encounter?
- What is the narrating voice's particular relationship to this subject at this point?
- What is the appropriate proximity of these subjects (topics) to one another right now?

On a basic structural level, I use the Four Ps — predicament, proximity, pacing, pattern — to assist me in determining each narrative's focus and form. Although these can occur in a different order, most often they follow this sequence. First, we identify and evoke the predicament that instigates the narrative and brings it into focus. Second, we intuit proximities that correspond with the narrative's unfolding. Third, after a period of inscription, we begin to assess if the pacing of the narrative's unfolding is accurate. Fourth, after a longer period of inscription, we evaluate what recurring patterns of images, key words/phrases, ideas, gestures/ actions, or sounds build and move the narrative forward, and then work more consciously with these patterns.

Proximity shifts are true to lived experience. They are our narrative's body language, and as such they can convey far more than words. Thus, it is our job as writers to recognize the inherent choreography of each narrative and the specific way it occupies its space — then recreate it on the page.

The Line

Does each narrative, whether it is prose or poetry, have its own distinct use of the line?

All lines require years of effort.

This simple line alone embodies years of learning about language, perception, construction of meaning, and the craft of writing.

The line is our loneliness.

> Line leans toward us — stretches its arms like a child.
> The line runs headlong to
> edge of prose page
> end of lyric line-break
> teetering momentarily there —
> like a pre-circumnavigation sailor —
> retreating to left margin's solid ground again.

Though the line is obsessed with keeping our attention — in truth, it is polymorphous — its reassurance is in touching the lines that precede and follow it. The line's instinct for nearness is confirmed by our basic gestures of inscription — the side of our hand smoothing the way for our words as we write in longhand across the page; our arm's rhythmic sweeping as we repeatedly return the typewriter's carriage; our hand's obsessive doodling motion as we navigate the screen with our computer mouse.

When we work with the line, we are working with one of our most generative forms. This is evidenced by the fact that *line*, when used as a noun, repeatedly appears as a key word in the vocabularies of math, art, hunting and sports, the military, surveying, genealogy, geography, science, commerce, systems of thought, transportation, power, and communication. The line connects us to our collectivity: it is our lifeline.

The line's shape can seem predictable. Our early grammatical training has created a standard sentence structure of noun phrase plus predicate phrase. Despite our use of repetitive line structure and unimaginative closed forms, the line's instinct is for surprise. The line may appear to be malleable and acquiescent to our habits, but it ventures into the unknown as soon as we trust it.

The line thrives on reinventing itself.

The shape of a thriving line is determined by its content, energy, and surrounding context. A line of similar structure, sound, and length can be the container for disparate content. In one context it is aggressive, in another euphoric or tender. Writers determine how to score words in a line with many of the same considerations composers use in the scoring of notes on a staff.

> When scored inaccurately,
> line's meaning — whether lyric or prose —
> is compromised.
> Its intention conflicted.
> Its sounding signals confused.

When our reader must read a line again and again in order to grasp our intended meaning, the scoring of that line is likely inaccurate, as it is when we read aloud from our work and find ourselves repeatedly stumbling in the same spot in a line. The line may be complex, but its clarity is its urgency. Confusion and awkwardness in a line build exponentially on one another. This is how the narrative gets derailed.

The line's core confidence is in touching its writer.

Its scoring must clone the movements of speech from its particular narrator or characters. Each speaker or narrator has an idiosyncratic speech signature distinct as one's own handwritten signature. The shape of each line — whether prose sentence or lyric line — is determined by: who is speaking (energy); what they are and are not saying (content); and to whom, when, and where they are speaking (context). Identifying and learning to inscribe each voice "signature" enables accurate scoring of each voice's lines. The reader knows exactly who is speaking with no need for a cue. This rare intimacy with a character's or narrator's voice enables the narrative's drama and meaning to unfolded naturally and inevitably by virtue of their very words.

The line generates story, not the writer's preconceptions about story. The etymology of *sentence* confirms this interdependency of a narrative's lines: *sentence, Latin sentire, to feel.*

> Line is emotional.
> Tactile. Like our hands —
> feels its way in the dark.

Line, Latin linea, thread, and Old English, cord, rope, series. When, as writers, we commit ourselves to writing a poem or prose piece, we must rappel down the cliff of our verbal vertigo. Hand over hand, we make our way toward a narrative ground we have only sensed. Word after word, we come closer to this untried ground we want solid footing on.

Scaffolding

Something is obfuscating or bogging down my narrative — what should I look for to figure out what it is?

Scaffolding is the necessary writing done during the inscription of our early drafts. It helps build narrative. Whether scaffolding is rudimentary and temporary or elaborate and erected for a considerable portion of our narrative, whether it manifests on the level of our line structure or on the level of paragraphs, stanzas, or chapters, all scaffolding must be removed in later drafts. If we fail to do so, scaffolding will inevitably overshadow the vivacity of the narrative. It quite literally deadens the narrative.

Scaffolding: 1. platform from which criminals are executed (hanged or beheaded).

In my experience, there are three different motivating factors that propel us to use scaffolding: notations, encodement, and laziness. Once we understand which of these motivations typifies us as writers, it then becomes far easier for us to identify scaffolding in our narratives. Of these three motivating factors, notation is likely the one of which we may already be aware. During inscription, when we sense or know that we are missing some aspects of the narrative, we may write passages and sections in a cursory manner. We do this to register that these bits must be fleshed out later; this scaffolding functions as a form of shorthand. When the writing is going well, when we are on the scent of the narrative, this is not the time to disengage from inscription to do the thinking, research, or experimentation required to flesh out these weak spots. The danger, of course, is that we overlook these areas later and fail to do the necessary additional work.

The second motivating factor is encodement. This is perhaps the most vexing of the three. Unlike notation, we most often are not aware we are using encodement. Encodement is just what it says. The narrative we write has areas that are encoded: only we can fill in the blanks; only we know what those puzzling traces and verbal gestures hold. These are the spots where the reader becomes confused, puzzled, even frustrated, for they keenly sense that they are being excluded. When readers of our works-in-progress say, "I don't understand what is happening," "You lost me here," or "Something is missing," they are most often correct. Encodement originates in the family and sometimes community. It works well among those who intimately share a narrative. It's one of those situations where one can finish another's sentence. Our readers are seldom in this category. When I mention encodement to a writer, he often replies, "But it's there!" When I ask him to show me exactly where "it is there," he is surprised to discover it isn't: it is there only in his own memory or imagination.

The third motivating factor is quite simply laziness. Perhaps, to be fair, it is not only laziness but also a subtle distrust of the reader's intelligence. This form of scaffolding will be recognizable in its stiff and often tedious tone and proximity. It functions as unnecessary commentary and explanation. A term I have coined and use often for it is "billboarding." The writer figuratively holds up a billboard that states things in a pedantic fashion. When we take the time to evoke the scene, dialogue, extended metaphor, or unique unfolding of an insight, the reader also enjoys the pleasures of getting it. We have kept her a part of how the narrative is generating itself.

Sometimes scaffolding may be referred to as "pre-writing": the writing you do, similar to warm-up stretching, before you go for a run or workout. I also think of it as a dog circling around before it lies down on the floor. The writer senses what the narrative requires, and is trying to find the way in. A dog circles because it instinctually remembers doing so in the wild to beat down the grass in order to lie down. We might also think of it as setting the stage; but, again, we need to remember that the narrative isn't stage setting but the interaction of the characters, thoughts, or images. Sometimes, our sophistication in writing scaffolding mimes the actual narrative. We can develop a fondness for it, but it eventually obstructs access to the narrative, weakens its focus and energy.

In my book *The Bat Had Blue Eyes*, I incorporated eight short Buddhist sutras that not only gave focus to the narrative but also drove the narrative forward to where it wanted to go. Trusting the comments of one of my reliable first readers, however, I later had to accept that all but one of these sutras needed to be deleted. At first it felt like prying the jewels out of the crown, but soon I could see that the narrative required an unadorned, solitary voice. Scaffolding, though vital to the creation of a narrative, ultimately strikes the reader as artifice, signage, a tangent, unnecessary.

Scaffolding: 2. a temporary platform used by workers in the construction, repair, or cleaning of a building.

Try identifying the scaffolding as you read the excerpt below, then assess how your reading experience changes in version two.

"Triple-Twenty" *(original draft)*
by Pat Buckna

There was nowhere to practise indoors at the Birkett Manor except in the basement, but the concrete walls quickly dulled the points of darts that missed and there was no telling what awful things might emerge from the dark crawl space. The apartment's brick exterior didn't work and it was strictly forbidden to hang the board on either of the two entrance doors. That left only the laundry platform: a tall wooden structure with stairs, handrails, and landing large enough to accommodate two women with full laundry baskets. Immediately below where they stood hung the large dartboard; twenty feet in front of them stood the young dartsman taking aim. Summers are short in Alberta and don't provide many days for either hanging laundry or perfecting triple-twenties.

Making a triple-twenty is simply a matter of concentration: grasping the thin dart at its balance point, concentrating on the landing spot, visualizing the slight arc of the dart when it leaves the hand, then waiting for the thwump as it lands — point buried, feathers trembling — right on target. Not all throws are successful; some fall low and to the left and earn only a single point, and a few actually fall short, landing in the dirt under the laundry platform. Over many days of practice, the wooden edges of the platform become pitted with a series of holes from errant darts, but generally more darts pierce the board than miss. One day, however, a young tenant from Apartment Two, standing on the platform with a dress in one hand and a pin in the other, let out a painful cry.

"The Laundry Platform" (revised after removal of scaffolding)

The young tenant from Apartment Seven had her hands full. She stood on the laundry platform and as she reached up to hang a wet undergarment on the clothesline, a dart came whizzing out of nowhere and stabbed her in the leg. A few feet away on the grass stood the caretaker's son, his arm lifted, fingers pointed towards the small dartboard that hung from a spike on the side of the laundry platform, directly below the young woman's feet. The instant the dart struck the young woman's leg, the slip she was pinning to the line fell like a wet rag and she let out a scream, which frightened the caretaker's son — the one who'd thrown the damn dart that had hit her in the leg.

When she pulled that damn dart from her leg, she saw the red bloodstain on the tip, the same red that now trickled down her leg towards her ankle. It must be lonely, she thought, for a child to live in this apartment filled with old people. She set the dart down on the platform beside her, wiped the blood from her leg then licked her finger. It tasted like tears ...

When writer Pat Buckna removed the scaffolding that comprised most of his original draft, he allowed the actual story to take the lead and unfold. The result is a far more compelling narrative that locates us inside the emotional and sensate experience of the boy, and this scene becomes vivid and achingly lonely.

Once you are aware of how scaffolding functions, you'll find it easy to identify and eliminate. This process may require minor cleaning — removing the opening line or two of a poem or the tempting punchline at the end of a poem — or it may call for a ruthless execution. One author I know had to remove 40 percent of her novel. The presence of scaffolding must be questioned in every piece of writing. It is not something we grow out of as writers. It is an ongoing part of the writing process. It is important, however, to reassure ourselves routinely that no effort is lost nor writing wasted during the scaffolding stage of inscription.

A caution. Do be careful to not delete a semi-conscious or conscious reclaiming of a device that might typically function as scaffolding. For example, Emily Dickinson's editor corrected her extensive use of dashes — later they were reinserted into her poems when it became apparent that Dickinson was intentionally reframing the function and effect of the dash — not realizing that this was one of her signature compositional strategies and a distinct aspect of her voice.

A reminder. Although scaffolding is a strategy you use in early drafts, sometimes you will find yourself introducing it during revisions. This happens when you are experiencing doubts about trusting your readers' acuity, when you are not confident in your narrative's ability to sustain the reader's attention, or when some vital aspect has gone unexplored in the narrative and simply needs to be further developed.

Depth of Field

What is diminishing the momentum of my narrative?

If you imagine a movie being shot entirely in close-up, or entirely in panorama, then you immediately begin to understand the problems experienced by the reader when the depth of field in a collection of poems, a memoir, or a novel is not being taken into account by the writer. Narratives that lack depth of field can be quite readily identified by their sameness of tone, texture, and tension, regardless of what is transpiring in the story.

For a moment, let's consider depth of field in relation to the evolution of interviews done on television. Early television programming was modelled on theatre and vaudeville. Viewers, accustomed to theatre and vaudeville's array of action, however, rapidly lost interest with the advent of interviews conducted with one stationary camera fixed on the seated interviewer and interviewee. In real conversations, we often look as much at what surrounds the person with whom we are talking, or we focus in and out, on different parts of the other person's face, body, clothes, and gestures. The subsequent invention of talk shows skillfully employed a range of depth of field via zoom, pan, and puncture when the host interacts directly with the audience.

In this book, depth of field became an increasing concern in the final two years of working on the manuscript. Although the essays vary — to some degree — in form and sensibility, I found that twenty-four essays in a row still made for a dense read with little time for absorption. More varied paces and pauses were needed. Eventually, I struck on the idea of folding in close-up, intimate vignettes excerpted from interviews done with me (dialogue), and written sketches of early-life incidents that shaped me as a writer (anecdotes).

Whether in a conversation or looking at art in a gallery, we inevitably move closer, step back, veer across the room, often return to look again, then finally depart. The movement back and forth between close-up and distance is deeply instinctual — we are doing it all the time — not only physically but also emotionally, mentally, and psychologically. Depth of field is how we perceive context, proportion, and proximity — hence meaning. It provides us with the pauses and different angles of seeing that we need in order to reflect, sort, and absorb. It is the basis of how we determine our relationship to everything; is how we "read" the nature of one another's relationships to everything.

As a writer, if you think of your text cinematically, then you can easily begin to look for these three basic depth of field positions/ locations:

- Distance/panorama (landscape, historical background, contextual backdrop)
- Middle ground (interaction between narrator and subjects such as people, places, events, ideas, objects; characters and subjects; "blocks" of concepts)
- Foreground/close-up (detail, intimate encounters, inner monologue, moments of understanding, synthesis, reverence)

"Hair" (excerpt)
by John Rich

It was a hair.
    A Hair.
    One Hair.
    Singular.
    Alone.

In itself such a small thing until it is mixed with its siblings giving the head shape, the body protection and warmth.

It was a long, blond, wavy hair with body, curl, and colour. Starry ringlet curls. It reminded her of Movie Star hair: she immediately had the image of Kim Basinger, in the movie *L.A Confidential*, but she couldn't say why. It could have been a stray piece of dental floss or some fishing line or thread … but it wasn't. It would have been unnoticeable, really, had it been sitting anywhere other than on top of Tom's black boots acting as a glowing contrast to their darkness. Hardly noticeable even then, had she not been straightening out the mat in the front hallway with her nose just inches from the boot's toe, hanging over it, suspended like a drop of water on the edge of a faucet the instant before it breaks free and plunges into the hard steel of the sink exploding in a thousand directions.

Her own hair was a dark brown bordering on black since birth, freshly dyed last week. She was too young for that touch of grey just yet. Tom's hair was black, always had been, straight and cut short after work on the first Thursday of every month for the last fifteen years.

Rich's choice of a shifting depth of field (proximities) allows him to evoke that particular slow-motion deductive back and forth coming-to-awareness process (which I call Approach — Retreat — Return) we go through when we unexpectedly are confronted with disturbing information.

When assessing your narrative's use of depth of field, consider changing the depth of field position to see what you discover. Take two pages that you feel dissatisfied about and identify the overriding depth of field position. For example, maybe it's mostly historically distanced. Shift the focus, rewrite it in close-up, and see what happens.

A lack of depth of field is indicative of a narrative making its case, whether emotionally or intellectually. These narratives are more concerned with reportage, description, expounding, proving than they are with evoking the subtleties and complexities in which interactions and insights actually unfold. These are commonly known as the "And then" narratives. We have all written them. We write them in a compulsive coma-like manner. Or, sometimes, we write them as a kind of notation preceding our first, fleshed-out draft. These flat-field narratives are hallmarked by relentless repetitions of line structure, pace, and sensibility: they are numbingly predictable. As often, however, the power of a well-rendered narrative is diminished, even dulled by small errors in depth of field. Occasionally, the depth of field remains stationary — if, for example, a narrator or character is deeply alienated from everything and everyone including himself. But this is rare. Constant repositioning seems to be the nature of our minds, hearts, and bodies.

It is possible, whether in an essay, poem, or novel, for the depth of field to be essentially accurate, but for proximity — in a specific area — to be inaccurate. Consider this example: A close-up of an intimate exchange between two lovers may need to accommodate one of them subtly repositioning herself in her mind to another time, place, and person (for whom she felt deeper love) of which her lover is unaware. In this case, the narrator and the character who remains in the present hold the depth of field in close-up, while the other character temporarily breaks away (via disassociating thoughts) to a different spatial proximity signalled by a change in body language, tone, or structure in her dialogue. As readers, we are not only provided with the correct signals, but we are also given the option to employ our own inferences.

Accurate depth of field embodies the shifting configurations or movements of lived experience and perceptual modes: it is a core spatial language that the reader instinctively recognizes, trusts. Enters.

The Table

Table, desk — does it matter which one I write on?

My writing tables have always been old, soft wood tables with a drawer or two tucked just beneath their tops. Over time, as I become familiar with their marks, scratches, and stains — the patina traces of previous owners — I am comforted by their hints of histories I will never know. Urged on by the countless hours others have toiled and been transported on this surface.

A table's grain is akin to currents of narrative. If we were to slice a narrative horizontally we would see its heartwood and concentric circles issuing outward toward the reader. Slicing it vertically, we would see how a narrative's variable currents — like a tree's reaching limbs, branches, convexities — take shape and implore the reader. Each time I sit down, my table reminds me that my role as writer is to navigate between the force fields of a narrative's horizontal and vertical coming into being.

Of all the objects in our contemporary life, the table is among the most ancient — dating back to prehistoric times. Its representation in visual art, however, has been curiously infrequent. Aside from Dutch still life paintings, our prominent visual template of table has been that of public feast (Hieronymus Bosch) and religious sacrifice (Leonardo da Vinci).

In contrast to the table's companion, the chair, the table has a direct relationship with Egyptian writing via ancient Roman codes incised on tables of stone, the Ten Commandments, early commerce records, and science and math reference tables. Yet our strongest association with the table is a domestic one. It is the site of meals, conversations, gaming, and the craftwork of hands. The saying "food for thought" indicates the reciprocal relationship between nourishment and language.

A table is open, versatile, feminine. The only other form I spend as many hours curled around is my lover's body. As writers, the table is our familiar. It is upon this intimacy with the table that we write our way into the public world of the tables as we prepare our manuscripts with publishers and editors, as we meet our readers as they acquire our books across bookstore counters and library lending counters, as students study our writing upon school and library desks.

Associations with the desk are almost exclusively those of the public realm: institutional sites of education, commerce, and governing. The desk, though more practical, is also more armoured: defended. I prefer a table with its embodiment of negative and positive space. Prefer its more inclusive lineage. Versatile and communal — from birthing table to mortician's slab; assembly line to altar — table holds and bridges our living. Indigenous wisdom believes that the backs of dogs and cats are our bridge between the domesticated and the untamed worlds. Four-legged table bridges the untamed creative instincts travelling down our arm to the paper or computer screen to our readers.

Table, Latin, tabula, board, list, a painted panel, map, writing tablet, document, plank. In the wood of the table we meet tree, as we meet it in pencil, page, chair, room, and books. This is a writer's lineage. *Tree, deru-, truth.*

The table upon which I began this essay was borrowed. Because its legs were too short, I placed it gently upon stacks of my hardcover reference books. For some time I hesitated about this double use of my books. But I could not afford to buy another table, so I tried it out. The experience awoke a new awareness in me — that these books literally supported my writing: table's legs taprooting into them.

A table is the pith of living: it deserves odes as one of our oldest, most steadfast companions.

In-fluencies # 2

I was named after my two grandmothers. From my mother's mother I was given my first name: Betsy. Grandma Hovey was paralyzed and rendered speechless by a severe stroke. From my father's mother I was given my second name: Barbara. Grandma Warland was never called by her proper name but rather by the nickname of Belle. It is a mystery how my grandmother had a French name as there wasn't a trace of French language or culture in our rural area. This was the grandma whose gestures signalled to me — like the clear ringing of a bell — that she knew who I was. Who, in her widowhood, would quietly listen in on her neighbours' conversation on her shared party phone line: one ring meant the call was for the Johnsons; two rings for the Olsons; three rings meant for the Larsons; four rings the Warlands.

Her eavesdropping was totally uncharacteristic. I think she did it because she was lonely and because she wanted to remain part of our community narrative, which newly widowed women suddenly found themselves less and less included in.

Mostly, she was silent in her eavesdropping. Occasionally, however, she would jump into her neighbours' conversations when she spotted an inaccuracy — providing the correct information — then return to silence again.

This was a revelation to me. There were other ways to navigate speech and silence; and later, words and blank spaces on the page.

Unpublished prose, by Betsy Warland, 2008.

Scored Space

How might my use of space on the page contribute to the meaning of my narrative?

White space is the writer's medium as much as the black lines of language.

The gravitational pull between the blank spaces and the inscribed spaces of narrative signifies the powerful role of scored space. The units of space between and around letters, words, and punctuation are the negative spaces of written language. Inscription is impossible without them, just as a table is not a table without absence. The lack of a solid form beneath the table — the open space in which chairs are moved in and out — defines the table's existence as much as wood, metal, plastic, Arborite, or glass. Negative spaces in a black-and-white photograph are as crucial to establishing meaning as positive spaces. Film noir's heightened use of darkness, shadow, and light created a form of narrative as important as plot and dialogue.

We might also think of scored space sculpturally — that a volume of words is dependent upon a corresponding volume of space just as a marble carving depends on the contrast of surrounding air. A drawing and a written narrative are even more similar in their necessitating a balance between spaces and markings.

All marking = indecipherable blackness.

Curiously, space refers to both tiny, incremental units as well as to the great masses — the universe itself. For centuries the printing press made space seem as concrete as the blank pieces of lead type used to separate words and characters.

Scored space, however, signals the dynamic, multi-dimensional world between the letters comprising each word, between each word, and between the narrative of words and — as Charles Olson defined it — their "field." As writers, we work within this energetic world — currenting among blank spaces, inscribed spaces, and the intimate environment they create between the writer and reader.

Every line of prose and poetry embodies this energy arcing back and forth between blank and inscribed space. Consequently, every line asks to be scored appropriately to convey the particular intervals, resonance, emphasis, and rhythm required by its narrative context.

In written narratives, inscribed scored space conveys an event, an image, a character, an idea, while blank scored space evokes the unknown, the unspeakable.

Scored space keeps us honest.

It signals and acknowledges the unknown, the unspeakable, the withheld, the censored, the assumed, the deleted, the gestured at, the taboo, the denied, the forgotten, the obliterated, the unrealized, and the beyond-language of the sacred.

One of the most interesting exercises I have created for exploring this different form of narrative is the Negative Space Poem, which can also be used with prose. The writer identifies a poem or section of prose in which he senses something is missing, then he literally writes into the negative space to see what it is silently hold-ing. This writing into may only require a few words — in the unmapped spaces — that anchor the poem or scene on a deeper level, or it may require many more words that include the reader in a subtle yet pivotal sequence of increasing intuitive awareness.

The following Negative Space Poem occupies the entirety of the previously existing poem's blank space, creating an appropriately claustrophobic sub-narrative. Notice how the writer, Eryn Holbrook, has inscribed the "meaningless" space of the page with the presence of the person whom the narrator is addressing, which in turn, draws the reader into a far greater sense of their shared, complex, claustrophobic history.

Do No Wrong   eryn holbrook

So uncomplicated So then say it again make it simple enough to understand
I should have known that you would love me anyway we are fading in & out
of these surface to air communications these war scenes shot at a distance.
Did you listen to the message that I left the other day? An urgent message
I'm sorry—I don't know what got into my head. then me forgetting to return
your call for 3 days in a row; could have been 4 but nobody's counting now.
You were always the one with the decency Scientifically speaking, there are
to give me what I needed as opposed very few wholes that can't be broken
to what I want. down into their composite parts (atoms & hearts included);
should we decide to make this exchange, the shock would destroy us both.
You don't have to pretend that you can You can depend on this sickness to
see beyond my imperfections— last well into the spring, but i am willing to
I'm as human as the next one. carry it over—the burden of your perfection.
Troubled by our falsely construed history, we are in it over our heads again
In my eyes you can do no wrong. we are in it because of what you've done.
In my eyes you can do no wrong you can do no wrong you can do no wrong
Why is this so simple? How do you pronounce this feeling in your language?
I wanted it to hurt more than this There is something like pain missing; is
I have emptied out the contents of my heart there is something like that left
to make room for you. here where I made up this room for you with blinds
pulled curtains drawn? No, there's nothing left of me here now that you are.

When we write, we are faced with the vast vocabulary of silence.

These irrefutable silences mean different things in different contexts at different times with different people. They convey as much as the inscribed text, cue the reader how to interpret the print on the page. Scored space is a language that is never neutral.

In the following prose text, writer Camilla Pickard scores her text to be faithful to the tension in this scene.

"*Man on a Red Sofa*"
by Camilla Pickard

I meet with him. It's in a coffee bar.

Plaster of Paris gods watch us. He asks too-personal questions about my life and I answer them all, all of them, truthfully, as if he'd recognize my lies.

Where did you grow up?
What's your family like?
Do you have a brother?
Your first boyfriend ...?
What kind of relationship do you have with your father?

So, you were — a good girl?

What has this got to do with filmmaking? Does it matter? I can't conceal anything, so he keeps asking. My opinions on sexuality, love, desire. Men I've enjoyed and disliked: their habits, affectations, their preferences. Like an embalmer, he removes everything from inside me, precise and tolerant: brain hooked out through the nose, viscera through the mouth. In two hours, he has possession of my secrets. He's made me his intimate friend.

The use of blank scored space signals the narrator's vulnerability when she suddenly finds herself being baited by a series of fly-fishing questions. Pickard's use of contrasting, densely inscribed space intensifies the sensation of the divulging narrator being reeled in.

Scored spaces of poetic lines, line and sentence placement and structure, stanza and paragraph breaks, fragmentary and continuous poetic and prose narratives create pacing and emphasis indicative of the nature of each narrative's particular requirement.

Historically in North America, the majority of writers, publishers, readers, and reviewers have appeared to be uncomfortable with prose writers who use compositionally scored space on the page. Just as the prospect of open spaces is alluring, we are equally anxious to fill them — especially with prose. With our compulsion to fill space, our writing often becomes a wall of words that drives our readers away, or at best, results in readers skimming countless stanzas and passages. Prose can be written in a way that is more porous, varied in pace, tone, and texture, leaving more room for the reader and narrative to interact with one another.

When I was about to send out my first solid draft of *Bloodroot: Tracing the Untelling of Motherloss*, I was advised by numerous literary friends that a publisher would never agree to the amount of scored space in the manuscript. To address this, I ran the entries together with asterisks between each entry. My first readers (in my case these are a few writers, a couple of editors, a visual artist, a librarian, and my brother) had difficulty reading it: they found it overwhelming. This was such an anomaly that I decided to reset the manuscript with its scored space intact, and this time they couldn't put the manuscript down.

Heightened awareness of how to score the resonant space of each poem, essay, or chapter opens up a mutually shared space in which the reader and writer are free to absorb what is being articulated, to discover our own emotions and illuminate our thoughts.

After thirty-some years of exploring and working with scored space, I came across this quote in a writer's manuscript I was working on. Although I sensed my experience of scored space tapped into an old wisdom, I was stunned when I read the following:

> The black fire are the written letters ... the white fire are the spaces on which the letters rest. The black letters represent the cognitive message, and the white space, that which goes beyond the cognitive idea. The black letters are limited; the white spaces catapult us into the realm of the endless, the limitless; it's the story, the song, and the silence.[1]

Meaning is interactive. Meaning accumulates and articulates itself in the tiny increments of a letter and a pause; a word and a poignant empty space.

---

1. Peninnah Schram, "Jewish Models Adapting Folktales for Telling Aloud" in Birch and Heckler, eds. *Who Says? Essays on Pivotal Issues in Contemporary Storytelling* (Little Rock: August House, 1996). As quoted in Ada Glustein, "Storied Voices: A Phenomeno-logical Study of Identity and Belonging" MA thesis, Simon Fraser University 2006. Quotation of the words of Rabbi Avi Weiss in the Talmudic commentaries.

Methods of Inscription and Composition

Why do I often lose interest when I am writing or revising a narrative?

As you inscribe and compose, there are always questions quizzically poised over the page about where you need to linger, deepen, extend, and where you need to economize, compress, and move on with the narrative. To engage creatively with these ever-present questions, you must become aware of your own methods of inscription. I have come to believe that there are two methods of inscription: subtractive and additive.

I have imported these two terms from visual art. It is helpful to hold in mind how these methodologies operate when applied to sculpting. Additive is quite simply the process of adding on. For example, if you are sculpting a head, you might build a wired armature of its rudimentary shape then begin to build on it with layers of papier mâché. Through this step-by-step additive process of layering on the face, jaws, nose, ears, mouth, eyebrows, cheeks, and hair take form. If you are sculpting a head in marble, however, you must use a subtractive method — chisel its features away from, or out of, a solid block of marble.

You are likely a subtractive writer if it is important for you to get it all down initially and not torment yourself with concerns about sequencing, proportion, and the suitability of everything you inscribe. You need to block in the entire canvas to establish what the narrative's territory seems to be. Once you have done this, you return to refine, delete, reconfigure your narrative through an extended series of revisions that often shrink the text as you revise, making it more focused and succinct. You may write new additions, too, but the essential activity is one of refinement and removal.

For an additive writer, however, it is necessary to revise as you inscribe — incrementally — fine-tuning before you move on. You find it impossible to write the second stanza of a poem or the second chapter of a novel until you have crafted the first one to your satisfaction. You move back and forth between inscription and composition as soon as you have written your first few words or lines of a narrative.

Like any guiding concepts, there are variations on these two basic modalities, as well as false indicators as to which one suits you best. The nature of some narratives requires both methodologies of inscription and/or composition at different stages of the writing process, or at different points in the sensibility of the narrative. Also, when we find ourselves bogged down during inscription, it is sometimes useful to reinvigorate ourselves by consciously switching to the other modality. Yet, for the most part, we will consistently inscribe in whichever of these two modalities suits us best. One is neither better nor more "writerly" than the other. What is crucial is that you realize and trust which method inherently works for you. You can spare yourself a lot of frustration by not assuming nor forcing yourself into one method when the other is a far better fit: one in which you are not working against your own grain but confidently with it.

But, you might ask, "Is my additive or subtractive inscription process a habit of personality or my inherent writerly one?" Personality, in fact, is not a reliable indicator. Those of us who are shy, concerned with perfection, anxious to pin things down, or preoccupied with using our time efficiently need to be cautious about assuming our inherent modality is additive. Writers who are highly susceptible to their inner critic, premature editing, or censoring themselves should be careful not to assume their inherent modality is additive.

On the other hand, if your personality is inclined to be extroverted, divulging, sometimes monologist, encyclopedic, concerned about productivity, or averse to authority, you need to refrain from automatically assuming that your inherent modality is subtractive. Writers who have an aversion to editing and revising, who shop around for too much feedback because they are unclear what their narratives are really about, who lose their momentum and abandon their narratives frequently, who maintain they don't have an inner critic should be cautious about assuming their style is subtractive.

It's not a bad sign if you find yourself saying, "What if I don't know which one I am?" It simply means that you are beginning to develop an awareness. Most poets, in particular, believe that the right way to inscribe poetry is additive. But for inherently subtractive writers, this can rein in their rhythms, lateral thinking, sense of form, and tonal range. When they discover that they are subtractive writers, their poems and forms become more energized, quirky, and often extended.

The guiding indicator, whether in inscription or composition, is sense of discovery. Discovery is what drives all writing. If you are only rarely experiencing discovery as you inscribe or compose, alter your method and see what happens.

Spatiotemporal Structural Strategies

How can I make the conditions from which my narrative springs more implicit?

Each narrative we write inhabits its own spatiotemporal environment. When we accurately evoke its peculiar confluence of time and space, its state of consciousness engages us deeply. My use of the adjective *peculiar* might seem odd, but peculiarity is precisely what attracts us to writing the narrative.

Regrettably, many promising contemporary narratives lack the necessary spatiotemporal structural strategies to saturate the reader with their peculiar environment. These narratives move along at the same pace and depth of encounter, and with the same intonation and textural tactility. A significant turn in the narrative is rendered in the same manner and with the same amount of text as an insignificant occurrence. We might liken this approach to a storyteller narrating her story in the same tone, with unchanging facial expression, body language, and timing. I think of it as a flattening out of narrative, a kind of reversion to 2-D that may be promoted by our ever-increasing reliance on virtual reality and electronic communication. A recent example of reduced reliability of 2-D communication is MIT's study that found that there is a 50 percent chance of a misunderstanding occurring in each email communication. This also happens in the exchange of letters, but there are more cues in letters — from type of paper and choice of inscription tool to the varying length. Time and timing also play an important interpretive role in successful communication: from the amount of time we devote to writing a message or letter to the passage of time before we receive it to the time we choose to sit down and read it and reread it.

Meaning is spatiotemporal and contextual. If I lean over and say, "I'm here" in your ear, contrasted to if I say it with a raised voice from another room, you automatically recognize that these are two very different statements. The sentence itself does not signal this. The spatiotemporal rendering is what cues us to the sentence's significance and meaning. It is not enough to put the sentence on the page: it must occupy — navigate — its peculiar spatiotemporal environment unerringly.

When I begin teaching a creative writing course, workshop, or retreat, I often hold up a blank sheet of paper and ask the writers to identify what it is. Initially, there is a bewildered and incredulous silence, then a flurry of obvious answers. To each I say, "Yes, but what else is it?" Then puzzlement increases on the writers' faces, even irritation, before they sense the necessity to drop to a deeper level of cognition. Sometimes it hits someone; more often it does not. But when I say "public space," the shock of recognition is palpable — almost akin to suddenly realizing that one's bedroom curtain is far more sheer than had been assumed.

After a brief discussion of the page as public space, and deline-ating the difference between a diary or journal page, which is private space, contrasted with the 8 1/2" x 11" sheet of paper as public space, I ask students to draw an overhead diagram of how they typically occupy a room in public space. Again, there is puzzlement, but their curiosity is piqued. I specify that it must be an enclosed space in which there is no pre-assigned seating. It could be a café, a bus, a theatre, a classroom — any kind of public room that they frequent. I instruct them to mark the location of doors, windows, furniture, and significant objects such as large potted plants, as well as where other people are located, and then to indicate where they routinely sit or stand. When we discuss each writer's diagram it is apparent — and often amusing — how habitual and predictable our patterns are in the ways that we do, and do not, occupy a room in public. A few basic templates appear every time: many writers, like dogs, prefer to be seated in a spot from which they can observe everyone in the room, and often this spot is close to one of the doors or windows. But there are also surprising, idiosyncratic diagrams.

One writer's diagram was of a party in which she located herself on the balcony. Another writer, who grew up as a foreigner in Thailand and was writing a manuscript about how these formative years shaped her, drew a diagram in a coffee shop where she is sitting with her back to everyone, looking out a large window. This diagram suggested to me that in her writing project, an interesting aspect of the narrative (besides her focus on the larger public world) is her unusual positioning to the domestic world — signalled by her back to everyone — which likely propelled her deep engagement with Thailand.

Another writer/visual artist's diagram was of an art opening where he entered the room and circled around its parameters, greeted various people, retreated outside to have a smoke, then re-entered the room and located himself near the centre in a conversation with a couple of people. This three-tiered structural approach to narrative shed light on strategies he needed to consciously employ and intensify in his narrative.

There are as many diagrams as there are writers. Even similar ones have their own idiosyncratic signatures. I urge you to use this method to gain insight into the structure of your narrative. If you do this exercise every so often, you may discover that you have more than one pattern of occupying public space and the page.

When discussing their diagrams, writers often see how their most habitual manner of occupying and not occupying public space influences how they routinely inhabit and refuse to inhabit the page, regardless of what each narrative requires. When understood, these habits of occupying public space and the page can be used selectively to anchor and shape our narratives. In the remainder of this essay, I will briefly consider a number of other spatiotemporal structural strategies that authors have used to great effect when their strategies correspond with the body language of the narrative itself.

Containment

What we loathe, what we long for: containment.

Containment is not only a compositional strategy; it also expresses the basic conditions within which we live. I am thinking not only about the large containers of family, community, society, country, world, universe, but also the container of our bodies — the physical, mind, spirit, personality, soul — as well as the containers of language, narrative, form, and the page. Developing an awareness of our relationships to containment socially, as well as containment formally, enables us to access the power of each narrative far more effectively.

Containment is often the predicament against which a narrative asserts itself and comes into being. For example, if central aspects of a narrative are too overpowering for the reader, then containment is needed. If subjects or characters become deeply destabilized, or are trapped in disparate situations, we can assuage the distress of these conditions through containment. Consider how the focus on detail in this excerpt pace the narrator's mounting fear.

"I Sit on the Porch"
by Colette Gagnon

I sit on the porch with my fresh clean dress pulled over my bandaged knees, pink socks like tender feelings. Little sighs.

The neighbour boy skips out from the back of his house, a hard boy, all angled with excitement. Hey, hey! he cries, there's an accident at the corner!

His mother bustles over from their front walk. Come along! she says, a little out of breath. He tugs at my dress, a rough boy, too rough to play with. I lift the hem above my knees. Poor thing, his mother clucks. Come on, she pulls me along. Let's go see what's happened.

Their excitement hurries us down the block, around the corner and into the backed-up traffic. A crowd gathers briskly in spite of the heat. The sirens are wailing above our heads. The smell of ice cream from the doorway of the Foodland Grocery overwhelms me, nearly makes me sick. No, please. I want to go home. The neighbour's hand is firm and greedy as she pulls us toward the crowd.

Stand aside, folks! Step away!

Murmurs overhead, then shouts explode. The quick legs thicken, press forward, sideways, as if they belong to one enormous body.

The neighbour tugs on my arm so hard that I begin to cry, but my voice gets lost amid the pant cuffs and rolled down stockings. I am squeezed through the legs to the edge of the curb where a thick, familiar smell pushes up against me. Blood floods the road, bodies lie there, open, pumping.

There is a long, blank pause.

An arm, a leg, no arms or legs, and no — yes — no, the smell of a thing's insides.

Compression

Virginia Woolf developed a compositional strategy I call "intensification through compression." Though similar to containment, this strategy is more related to seamlessness, splicing, interfacing, stacking; it allows the narrative not to be limited by the measure of linear time. In her 1931 book *The Waves*, the passage of time is depicted through the interior monologues of six characters, and coherence is achieved via recurrent imagery and symbols. Woolf creates a form of narrative consisting of a series of impressions, unresolved vignettes that unfold in a seemingly random series of actions much like lived experience. This is how Woolf defined one of her most notable signature compositional strategies in *A Writer's Diary*:

> What it wants is presumably unity [*The Waves*] ... Suppose I could run all the scenes together more? — by rhythms chiefly. So as to avoid those cuts; so as to make the blood run like a torrent from end to end — I don't want the waste

that the breaks give; I want to avoid chapters; that indeed is my achievement, if any, here: a saturated unchopped completeness; changes of scenes, of mind, of person, done without spilling a drop.[1]

Compression can also mirror the non-stop switchboard of our mind, rapidly patching together disparate times, cultures, countries, geographies, histories, and personal responses, as in this excerpt from Lori McNulty's work-in-progress.

"*The Petrified Dancers*"
by Lori McNulty

This can't be. Vasanti's servant arrives holding out a tray of tea, eyes fixed to the screen. The deep-throated British announcer's voice has gone dry.... No one can say how ... it appears to be ... under attack ... we're hearing reports ... debris coming down ... a third hijacked ... filling with smoke ... terrible accident ... collapse.

By the time word reaches us the event is a story. Not here. Where? Humid air thick on my tongue. Too hot for sleeves. Now Vasanti and Rajkumar shift side to side, shaking their heads, as if they can almost see, already link events in a long historical chain. The worst in American history ... Bombay ... 260 dead ... firebomb ... hail of gunfire ... unprovoked attack ... car bombs ... border war ... bloody massacre....

---

1. Virginia Woolf, *A Writer's Diary* (Frogmore, St Albans: Triad/Panther Books, 1979).

Extension

Like E.M. Forster, we may be drawn to the strategy of extension, or expansion. Forster typified this approach as the difference between a writer who "may parallel our sufferings but can never extend them — and a writer who does extend them."[2] For Forster, great novels achieve an ideal of beauty, of freedom that may be most akin to our experience of music resonating outward with a greater sense of human existence: "Expansion. That is the idea the novelist must cling to. Not completion. Not rounding off but opening out."[3]

In my own poetry, I often use extension by allowing the poem to occupy the entire page — with its hesitancies, nuance and resonance, time-lapse of cause and effect — opening itself to the reader. Sometimes, in order to be faithful to the narrative, I will use extension in contrast to containment, as in this excerpt from my long poem in *only this blue*.

the course?

       water plummets
               — not knowing, not knowing —

      , she stands

                    on viewing platform
not knowing, not
knowing

---

2. E.M. Forster, *Aspects of the Novel* (New York: Harcourt, Brace and Company, 1927).
3. E.M. Forster, *Aspects of the Novel* (New York: Harcourt, Brace and Company, 1927).

camera expects a casual pose
insisting sameness
in every situation

inside the viewfinder
a green & red light
inform photographer
whether subject
is in or out
of focus

                    through the past three seasons she
         absent
             from rectangle story

                              , now

       — goes through the motions —

                    body as porous as water air leaf

Contiguity

Contiguity is defined as "sharing an edge or boundary" and "near; next (to) in space or time." Thus, narratives from different linear times, perspectives, and sensibilities can share contiguous space. Their adjacency may be conceptual, metaphoric, or emotive. With their adjacency, we see how they shed light on each other via their

breathing

contrasts or surprising similarities. We see how they interrelate far more than linear time or compartmentalized knowledge would ever suggest.

Contiguity is a contemporary way of life: we experience it daily via surfing the web and two hundred channels on our television. Contiguous forms of narratives that you may have written in or encountered as a reader are blended, braided, text within a text, collage, and parallel texts narratives. My 1987 book *serpent (w)rite* is a contiguous long poem that investigates and retells the first three chapters of Genesis. It incorporates excerpts from nearly a hundred disparate books from antiquity to the 1980s. Consider this one-page excerpt from "turn one."

Adam's words name

Eve's words repeat
(lip service)
she took the words right out of his mouth

this is how we acquired language
religion or myth it is our narrative
our incessant story line
script, to cut, separate, Scripture, manuscript,
riddle, discriminate, secrete, crisis

"Language exists in the form of a sum of impressions   Saussure
deposited in the brain of each member of a community, almost like a dictionary of which identical copies
have been distributed to each individual."

"The dictionary presents a world view, the bilingual   Hijinian
dictionary doubles that, presents two."
Eve taking the *bite, bheid-, bait*
"the story of Eve is also the story of the displacing of   Phillips
the Goddess whose name is taken from a form of the
Hebrew verb "to be" by the masculine God, Yaweh,
whose name has the same derivation."

The byte the basic unit of information
in our new language

Vacuity

With vacuity, I think of emptiness, void, isolation, loss, listlessness.
This spatiotemporal state is one of the more challenging ones to
evoke: its very nature seems to defy materiality. Poetry may be
the most suitable form for evoking this state, as the very form of the
poem acknowledges that vacuity is a powerful force that imprints
itself on us, signifies one of the stigmata of the human condition.
Prose writers also find some effective strategies for evoking vacuity.
Nicole Brossard's use of fragments, short narrative passages, and
contrasts against blank space is one example. In Miriam Toews's
novel *a complicated kindness*, the narrator's mother has inexplicably
left. The father's gradual depopulating of the furniture in the house
is an evocative metaphor for the loss of home and domestic comfort.
In Jamaica Kincaid's *The Autobiography of My Mother*, the very
title signals the impossibility of its telling. Kincaid's remarkable
sentence structure frequently begins with an assertion of being,

only to unravel into contradiction and antimatter by the end of the sentence.

Expansion and Contraction

In a recent article on author Anne Michaels and her novel *The Winter Vault*, journalist Gerald Hannon recounts:

> In prose, writer and reader are travelling through hundreds of pages together, and Michaels says it's important to slow the momentum down occasionally. "Music does that naturally, especially in a long symphonic work. It's the same thing with a novel, [there must be] moments built into the text to allow the reader to pause, to think, and to feel. From beginning to end, a book has to make space for the reader."[4]

Frankly, I was elated to read this because so few writers ever speak of (or seem to even think about) pacing and making room for the reader. Nor do many writers appear to be concerned about the narrative's requirements for places of expansion and places of contraction. I believe most narratives, regardless of genre, require this. Just as our bodies' countless functions depend upon expansion and contraction, so do our perceptual processes — whether mental, emotional, or spiritual.

---

4. Gerald Hannon, "Hiding in Plain Sight," *Quill & Quire*, April 2009.

Formally, expansion and contraction can be used for a wide array of effects. In the excerpt below from Arleen Paré's *Paper Trail*, note how Paré uses two-line paragraphs periodically to manifest the force of her father's sheer will. This contrasts with her use of expansive paragraphs with sentences that read like one run-on sentence to evoke her father's greater ambitions.

"*Paper Trail*"
by Arleen Paré

How my father would say: As the twig is bent, so grows the tree. Pliable and bent. Like me.

If something's worth doing, it's worth doing well. Workaholic and spent. Like him.

How elocution lessons were so important. That he took elocution when he was thirteen, his last year of schooling. He stood in the kitchen in his black business shoes, his mouth a perfect O articulating the second syllable of the word *el-O-cution*, his eyes steady on me. Asked if I ever got elocution in school. I only knew to tell him no. The strangeness of that word: elocution, like electric shock or electric chair or execution; electrocution, part elephant, part locomotion. He said it made all the difference, those lessons, when he turned thirteen, in elocution.

How he wished he'd gone into politics. Ever think of it? he'd ask, of going into politics ... or medicine? How, though he asked me, I knew he meant him. No chance for him, leaving school so young. Working at anything until he came to America. Then working and working. At anything. Making sinks for Crane Inc. when he didn't know a thing about them. Driving a horse-drawn bakery truck door-to-door in Montreal ice storms, the old brown horse skidding down the icy streets, falling down the hills.

Selling soap. Selling machines. Selling dances. Selling wax. Selling. Anything. He said.[5]

Excess and Fixed Points

In prose narratives, particularly those that evoke excess, unrelenting intensity, or chaos, a fixed point is frequently required — much like a bathtub drain — around which the series of dramas involving characters swirl or orbit. A fixed point might be a repeating metaphor, phrase, or gesture; a simple, stable element such as a location; or an abiding character or person who anchors the action. Fixed points provide contrast and depth of field. They also provide crucial pacing for the reader: spots in which the reader may literally catch his breath and absorb what is transpiring. In this way, fixed points provide a kind of physics of narrative.

In Di Brandt's first book, *questions i asked my mother*, she created an almost hyperventilating poetic prose line of excess that evoked the irrepressible curiosity of a young Mennonite girl at anxiety-provoking odds with her stoic and often-resistant mother and father.

Like narrative, we spend our entire life finding out what our compositional strategies are for telling a story. Spatiotemporal structural strategies, when used accurately and consciously, enable

---

5. Arleen Paré, *Paper Trail* (Edmonton: NeWest Press, 2007).

our narratives to evoke precisely how perception occurs within their set of idiosyncratic, unfolding circumstances. Think about your favourite authors and recall the deep pleasure and familiar anticipation you feel when you encounter their signature compositional strategies. Spatiotemporal structural strategies can become part of your signature writing style, as well as generative sources during the inscription stage.

In-fluencies # 3

he did write a letter once

when i was thirteen or fourteen and away at Y.W.C.A. camp. my mother was traveling with her sisters to the World's Fair in Seattle. it was a very short letter — maybe seven or eight sentences. he wrote it because my grandmother, his mom, had fallen and broken her hip and was in hospital. he felt i should know. she and i were very close. so were they and i think he was scared. his handwriting was large and curvilinear. very different from my college-educated mother's which was precise and tight. his sentences were very simple. i felt his innocence in the written word. it was painful to read that letter. i knew how hard it must have been for him to write it, the words came out in short staccato bursts like someone who was trying to speak after running a very long way.

Proper Deafinitions, by Betsy Warland, 1990.

Proportion

Why is my reader not noticing, or misinterpreting, significant parts of my narrative?

Proportion is the distribution of the weight and mass of a narrative's elements that shape its meaning. Proportion is not governed by predetermined linearity, logic, or even formula or plot but rather by how the experiencing of each event or insight takes hold. Our bodies are the mediators of proportion. It is the logic of our bodies that understands the relationship between meaning and proportion. It is our body that signals us when to change an expected or assumed scale to a scale that more accurately registers the felt experience in the narrative.

One writer with whom I worked was writing about hiking the Himalayas. Evoking a landscape of such magnitude is always a challenge. She had mostly succeeded, yet the narrative came across in a two-dimensional way. I encouraged her to locate the reader inside the body, mind, and emotions of the hiker, as well as to bring the reader close to her encounters with those she was hiking with and with the residents she encountered along the way. Adding this to her narrative made all the difference: it no longer had an impressive yet strangely distancing feel. Instead it became a visceral, emotive, sometimes deeply meditative reading experience. The reader might anticipate that the most compelling aspect of this narrative would be the stunning panorama, but in fact the actual step-by-step experience of such an arduous trek held the greater narrative weight. Proportion. The reversal of the expected proportional contrast was what enabled this narrative to take the reader where he had never been before.

Curiously, the foreground of a narrative does not necessarily determine its actual proportional weight or mass. An action or event in the foreground may not carry the substantial weight or mass. A literal "background" image can be a pivotal, unanticipated shift and suddenly steal the show from what seems to be the narrative's focus. The weight of the language and the mass of the stanzas/ paragraphs or scored blank spaces must reflect this.

When reviewing how to establish correct balance in the narrative, your internal critic must stand aside. It is only then that you are free to concentrate on identifying concerns of proportion such as: How are these central images building on and illuminating one another? Have I given them their deserved proportion and arresting power? Proportion is not just how much text is allotted to an event, character, idea, or image. Often we over-inscribe what we believe to be most important, amplify it to make certain the reader gets it. As in life, so on the page. Over-articulation can quickly slip into rant, melodrama, sentimentality, or directives.

Is it really necessary to assess and adjust proportion consciously? Wouldn't this just come naturally? Occasionally it does; more often, it doesn't. As composers or painters must establish a compositional balance among all the elements of each of their works, so must we writers. When we take the time to render proportion accurately, the narrative that may have been of interest to a reader then becomes the narrative that enters and haunts the reader. E.M. Forster, in his book *Aspects of the Novel*, devised a useful concept to assist him in giving appropriate proportion to the characters in his novels. The major, developed characters were *round characters*; the minor, gestural characters were *flat characters*.

Problems of proportion can often be traced back to inscription strategies used in early drafts that were necessary for sketching the narrative in. When writing a poem, the first draft is often inscribed intuitively. As you revise, identify the poem's central images, metaphor, and patterns. Frequently, these are obscured by unnecessary explanatory passages resulting from lack of conviction that the poem is effectively unfolding. Or these disproportionate phrases and passages may be due to a preliminary casting of a wide net to find what the poem needs. An incident, extended description or metaphor, explanatory passage, or character naturally diminishes, or increases, in importance as your narrative seizes its own life. Typically, the proportion of these original narrative elements will need to be readjusted in later drafts.

In-fluencies # 4

Our mother had an imaginative relationship to truth.

She didn't out & out lie, she rearranged a story's parts like some-one moving furniture in a motel room. It was presentation: how it looked to others. This was the basis of how it then looked to her.

Truth cut in half reveals itself.

As her daughter, I hated the liberties she took. With her cut & paste editing she had little regard for others' feelings. I couldn't, however, think of her as a liar.

I still can't. I thought of her as afraid; then, much later, I grew to think of her as a remarkable metaphorist.

Bloodroot: Tracing the Untelling of Motherloss, by Betsy Warland, 2000.

The Written Word

What is it about working with written words that endlessly intrigues?

The written word is our declarative mark left for others.

Just as a dog exhales warm breath onto blade of grass — reactivating a scent-message left by previous dog — the reader's eyes focus on the word, reactivating the written message left by its writer.

A written word — comprised of inscribed alphabetic letters — is a locus of visual symbols that represent speech, thought, emotion, culture, and history. Most of the letters of our phonetically based alphabet originated among the Phoenicians, Semites, and Palestinians as graphic sign-words around 1000 BC. If we look at the word *door*, for example, the *d* represented *door*, the *o* represented *eye*, and the *r* represented *head*. These graphic sign-words can function, along with contemporary usage, as a double encoding of meaning.

Word, wer-, to speak.

This double encoding also occurs when words mimic the sounds they represent, such as *cuckoo*, *snap*, *spark*. Known as onomatopoeia, this language process indicates how inherent sounds play a role in creating words.

A word is a semantic-stream we drink from.

Semantic-streams include: personal streams, in which a word like *house* contains the specific houses each writer and reader has known; collective streams, such as the word *earth*, which contains the meanings of how the earth has been recalled, experienced, and understood in one's lifetime; and linguistic streams, which reveal the etymological lineage of a word, its word relatives, and its historical context.

A word has almost no meaning in itself.

A word is dependant upon surrounding words for its meaning. Just as the specific meaning — context and emphasis — of a spoken word is established by gesture, intonation, facial expression, and the words surrounding it, so a written word's particular definition and causality is established by its surrounding words (context) and the scoring (intonation and gesture) of the line it occupies.

Tone, timing, embedment, historical context — personal and public — reveal the interdependence and mutability of words. The word *love* may seem to possess a fixed, even indisputable, definition. When, however, it is embedded in disparate narrative or lyric contexts — even in the single-word line or sentence "Love" — its fluid instability quickly becomes apparent. It can connote tenderness, seduction, a command, an endearment, an accusation, reassurance, a demand for reciprocity, a confession, a longing, or a smokescreen. Its meaning is entirely dependent upon its context and emphasis.

The ecology of words is acutely interdependent.

Words begin as sensations, a distinct feeling in our bodies, then they offer themselves to us as we search out the right words among the many offered, initiating specific movements in our hands as we inscribe these right words in the right order on a page.

Rereading, our bodies listen through sensation, emotion, and perception to the words we have just written — revising, reading, listening, sensing, revising, and re-sensing until the text is replete. This can take a few minutes; this can take a few years; this can take a lifetime.

Our written words are then reabsorbed into our bodies and the readers' bodies again. And again. It is through this process written words are continually enlivened to propagate other texts.

As new words are created, old words fall into disuse and die. The word *utter*, prior to our contemporary usage, meant "To publish (a book or the like)" and "To sell or deliver (merchandise) in trading."

Words are fluid, stiff, soft, sharp, opaque, hard, sticky, smooth, radiant, transparent, raw, polished, rough, reflective, slippery, cold, wet, hot, dry, murky, hollow, dense, resounding. Most words can embody many of these seemingly incompatible qualities. It is a mystery how words, though utterly interdependent and mutable, nevertheless possess an inherent integrity.

Words' preference for accuracy is what prompts readers and writers to question the veracity of what they read and write, to notice the signals words send when they don't ring true.

Contemporary definitions, as well as the etymological lineages of a word, denote almost exclusively verbal, spoken references. No word specifically and solely describes the phenomenon of the written word. Our inscribed units of alphabetic thought, memory, and emotion essentially remain nameless, even though our definitions of alphabet are entirely writing-based. Perhaps the narratives that have the most impact on us are the ones that encounter both language sites: oral (mouth) and written (hand).

Synapses of words — nerve fibre and signal — arc endlessly.

Nose to Nose: Poetry

Do poetry and prose really have disparate narrative roots?

With iambs of our infant breathing, rhythmic cycles of our bodily functions, patterns of sound and motion within our domestic surroundings, repetitive song of our distinctive crying, and comforting melodies of our parents' voices, poetry embraces us into our being here.

The structure of a poem is before, after, inside, and outside of words. We call it rhythm, rhyme, pattern, meter, cadence, tone. We call it the poem's musicality, form, impulse.

Poem is wave.

At poem's baseline is our unknowing, at its crest, the gathering of our knowing — the force between baseline and crest is the poem's momentum taking form.

Because a poem's very form acknowledges both what can be said or known and what can never be said nor known, poetry may be as close as we come through language to the sacred.

Lyric form is the lineage of poetry, as it is of sacred and mystical texts.

Poems that prick our imagination from generation to generation structurally encounter the known and unknown: this is the lineage pulsing within us.

Poetry, as music, is intrinsically an airborne art form: a poem must navigate page like a voice in space. Contemporary poetry often appears to be a visual art form, yet the most compelling poems integrate sound and sight.

When hearing a poem in a language from a culture we do not know, full comprehension remains out of reach. Unlike prose, however, a poem's signalling power is nevertheless operative. Poems transmit the sentiments of their sonic territories via each poem's unique set of emotive tones and narrative energy, and we are affected on a cellular level. A poem speaks to us in the same way that foreign music and visual art get through to us.

The body breathes the poem breathes the page.

When a poem and the poet's body share a profound intimacy, poem and page become lovers — nose to nose — inhaling/exhaling one another's breath.

Scored spaces inhale.

Scored lines exhale.

Most inscribed systems we have devised to represent meaning — written language, science notation, sheet music, math, and a number of the visual arts — rely on a related progression of configured lines and spaces. In poetry, blank scored spaces and inscribed lines converge: have comparable entitlement.

Language evidences our separateness.

Silence evidences what we share.

A poem's inscribed spaces may mean different things to different people, but these meanings do not need to be specified. We share them. The uninscribed space of the page is a powerful form of communication, as is silence: often both are mistaken for emptiness, excess, or something extrinsic.

Silence and space potentially hold all language and meaning.

Language acknowledges our separateness by insisting on telling us something specific. It is generated from our desire to connect, or to bridge a sensed gap in memory, perception, or feeling.

Poetry is a riptide where language and silence negotiate one another's equally powerful currents.

Ultimately, sound (language) and silence (scored space) are the same thing: emphasis and meaning.

Accurate scoring of a poem is critical. If the inscribed poem remains faithful to the intonation, pausing, emphasis, and rhythm of its oral expression, then its meaning is vivified. As in a piece of music, accurate scoring enables readers to see, breathe, and speak the poem as composed, delivering readers soundly into their own interpretations.

The integrity of a poem hinges on its set of specific circumstances. Just as a composer tends to write choral music to move through a cathedral's time and space, or a lullaby to move through domestic time and space, so the poet composes each poem. These circumstances invite us in; without them poetry remains obscured, closed.

Within its particular time and space, a poem is liberated to gesture toward, hint at. It is a sketch. A note. A brush stroke.

Poetry arouses us via devotion to articulating sensation, uncoiling perception — not by proof or explanation.

A poem is porous.

Scored pauses within a poem create openings for anticipation, exchanged glances, and exclamation.

Scored stanza breaks allow time for the reader's recognition of her own associations, thoughts.

A poem is a field of molecular word activity. The poet senses what is *already there*[1] and navigates accordingly. If we travail faithfully, we can return years later and be startled by a poem's wisdom, insight, beauty — of which we were not fully cognizant before.

---

1. When I wrote this essay in 1998–1999, I had not yet come across Frank Bidart's comment on Coleridge's concept of organic form: "Form must embody what is already there" (see "Embodiment").

Poetry is change in the act of. Like beauty, its fluidity surprises and transforms us. As with species' survival, poetry embodies resilient inventiveness.

A poem enters your heart the way an idea enters your mind.

Although poetry has narrative elements, its instincts and lineage are distinct from prose narrative's instincts and lineage.

Prose takes us on a journey.

Poetry may be the journey.

Intrinsic Form

How do I determine if I have found the right form for my narrative?

Everything is form.

Form is everything and therefore seemingly nothing.

Form can be so specific as to appear amorphous. Or it can be easily recognized and predictable. The use of the term *form* itself can contribute to our confusion: it refers to everything from the smallest details of crafting a text to the actual shape of a text to the literary form (genre) a narrative is written in. Typically, our interest in form pivots around questions of craft, such as: Is this extended metaphor working? Is this character underdeveloped? I call these *explicit form concerns*. Much has been written about them.

Explicit form is comprised of:

- genre (closed and open)
- chapters, sections, suites
- dialogue
- monologue
- metaphor and image
- traditional (or closed) rhyme and meter
- character
- narrator
- plot
- point of view and person (first, second, and third person)

But what of the more enigmatic questions about form, the less tangible challenges we must identify and meet to realize the full power of our narratives? Questions about intrinsic form are not as measurable, chartable, nor teachable as those of explicit form. It is easier to analyze why a character is not believable than to figure out why your narrative has lost its momentum, why everyone who has read your short story misread its key scene. These are intrinsic form concerns. Little has been written about them.

Intrinsic form is comprised of:

- words
- fonts
- syntax
- each line (structure and movement)
- each stanza (structure and movement)
- each paragraph (structure and movement)
- each scored space (white space on page)
- each inscribed space (black print)
- the entirety of each page of text
- the entirety of each piece (suite of poems, chapter of prose)
- the entirety of the complete text
- the field of context for the text

When you initially focus on intrinsic form, you may be bewildered by its enigmatic nature. This metaphor might be of assistance: if you build a house, you must decide upon its location, size, floor plan, approximate cost, and contractor. These are all explicit form concerns. Then you must make a thousand other daunting decisions: where to position it on the lot; what kind of shingles to use, which colour to paint the kitchen, what light fixtures to install, what kind of doorknobs to purchase. These are intrinsic form concerns. Initially, they seem not as significant.

Try this exercise in which you ask yourself to identify a word or phrase that embodies the specific way your narrative constitutes itself. You may need to ask yourself this question several times before you find an accurate word or phrase. One writer with whom I did this exercise first replied that her narrative constituted itself in a fragmented manner. I replied that this was too general: countless narratives build themselves this way. Eventually she arrived at a far more precise and evocative phrase: "a dismembered narrative." This phrase grabbed me by the collar with its veracity.

The second part of the exercise is to ask yourself to come up with a word or phrase that conveys exactly how the narrative expresses itself, lives itself out. The same writer initially came up with the word *love*. Again, I replied this was too general. Then, after some tries and discussion we agreed that it expressed itself through "sabotage" (historical, familial, self-sabotage). Later, this writer also identified the word that most definitively named her methodology: *sifting*. She had an enormous amount of material — documents, interviews, journals, articles, recorded conversations, photos, fictionalized accounts, dreams, therapeutic work — but now she possessed clear understanding upon which to base her decisions. Ultimately, these are the decisions that make all the difference.

Form = Content / Content = Form.

The Structuralists' conceptual adage "Form = Content / Content = Form" is one of the few contemporary principles that helps us assess intrinsic form. It was Aristotle, however, who first articulated intrinsic form. He maintained that form is not synonymous with structure but rather that inherent form informs structure. American poet Denise Levertov refers to the appropriate coupling of form and content as "fidelity to experience."[1] Although we may not know the reason, we do respond to this fidelity; we feel a kind of elation when we encounter a seamlessness of form and narrative. Why? Because nothing gets in the way — no artifice, no interpolation, no unintended awkwardness — and we are free to absorb these narratives: they saturate us, they inhabit us. As a result, we recall them vividly for years.

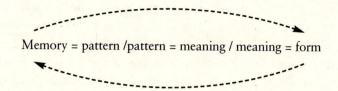

Memory = pattern /pattern = meaning / meaning = form

When meaning and like-minded pattern mirror one another, they create integrated form. This form enables us to write (recognize, retain, and store memory) then later enable our readers to read (retrieve this memory). When we fine-tune the narrative's intrinsic form, our readers re-experience the dynamic chain reaction, as seen in the diagram above, that sourced and inspired the narrative as if it were their own.

---

1. Denise Levertov, *New and Selected Essays* (New York: A New Direction Book, 1992).

Everything is memory: everything is form.

A concrete example of the intrinsic form process is the way our shoes are infused with our scent, imprinted with the contours of how our feet meet the ground. Our shoes remember our bodies. In turn, our shoes remind our bodies of who we are each time we wear them. When we compose with fidelity to experience, the narrative — which depends on various kinds of memory — becomes the form.

Our ability to remember is dependent on breath. Our breath has an extensive vocabulary that mimetically expresses different states of memory. Sighs, held breath, slowed breath, shallow breath, rapid breath, ragged breath, loud breath are just some of the breaths we choose to express memory, sometimes without uttering or inscribing a single word. As writers, our breath is one of our main guides and basic tools for inscription, composition, and revisions. Accessing it is not automatic. It takes practice.

The best way to begin is to try checking your breathing against your narrative's intrinsic form. Read aloud two pages of your work and pay close attention to how your breathing corresponds to the narrative's content. Are you running out of breath in an area where the narrative is tranquil? Is your breathing erratic where the narrative is taking you through some awkward, disorienting shifts? Focusing on this correspondence, or lack of correspondence, can help you fine-tune intrinsic form.

Memory as metaphor.

Coleridge suggested that form must embody what is already there. But what is already there must be recognized and be illuminated by the writer. I encourage writers to think of memory as metaphor. In *A Writer's Diary*, Virginia Woolf gives us a glimpse of this understanding when she reflects on her early inklings of writing *Mrs. Dalloway*:

> Yet I am now haunted by the semi-mystic very profound life of a woman, which shall all be told on one occasion; and the time shall be utterly obliterated; future shall somehow blossom out of the past. One incident — say the fall of a flower — might contain it. My theory being that the actual event practically does not exist — nor time either.[2]

Since it is impossible to recall the entirety of an event or experience, we must select, consciously or unconsciously, the aspects most significant to us, including sensation and interpretation. This inevitable selective memory is illustrated when several people who shared the same experience recall it differently only moments later — as evidenced by witnesses' disparate accounts at the scene of an accident. One writer writing a novel based on autobiographical material was well into a second draft when he happened upon his journals written during the period that inspired his narrative. He was shocked to discover that his journals contradicted his memory about very significant events. For example, he was certain that he had driven his lover to catch a plane and initiated their breakup on the way to the airport. In his journal, it was she who initiated the

---

2. Virginia Woolf, *A Writer's Diary* (Frogmore, St. Albans: Triad/Panther Books Press, 1978).

breakup on the way to the airport. I suggested to him that apparent action isn't always the most authentic action: he may have passively orchestrated their breakup (and this is the intention he remembered) though, on the surface, it was his lover who broke up with him. This is an example of where our poetic licence as writers is crucial. Our evoking of emotional truth is often more respectful of the narrative's integrity than factual truth is. This, however, must be done consciously and ethically.

"Meaning is not attached to detail ... meaning is revealed."[3]

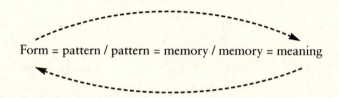

Form = pattern / pattern = memory / memory = meaning

This requires that the writer be fully embodied/present throughout the writing process. If she is not, or is only partially or periodically embodied/present, so will be the narrative, and so will be the reader. The writer's body is the site of all memory storage, research, imagination, processing, and selection: it is the conduit from which the narrative emits.

An intriguing way to explore how you might better maximize form = meaning is to take an excerpt, short piece, or poem and

3. Patricia Hampl, *I Could Tell You Stories* (New York and London: W.W. Norton & Company, 1999).

re-score it into three different forms. Allow the subtleties, subtexts, and tonal energy embedded in the writing to cue you as to options you have in rescoring it into three diverse forms/ versions. Don't be restricted by the pre-existing formal approach: try anything that frees the narrative to occupy the stage (page) in its full power.

Form = Memory

I believe the majority of problems we encounter as writers are ones of intrinsic form; torments about the merits of our subjects or inscription skills may often be misguided. In focusing only on explicit form, we seldom address the underlying problem — inappropriate use of intrinsic form.

The extensive use of free or open forms in contemporary poetry has contributed to our lack of understanding of intrinsic form. I say this as a free-form poet. It has produced several generations of poets who believe they are working in free or open form, but who are tightly noosed by their own unexamined and individualized closed forms. Prose writers, with some notable exceptions such as lyric prose writers, typically continue to use the traditional forms with little questioning; most contemporary prose writers and poets might be said to be inscribing in a formal trance.

When leafing through literary journals, anthologies, and contemporary books of prose and poetry, if you ignore the content and authors' names and focus only on the shape and obvious form used in each piece of prose and poetry, soon it becomes evident how formally conservative and limited contemporary writing is. A small handful of templates is used repeatedly. Given the fact that for poets there are over seven hundred traditional closed poem forms from which to establish fidelity of form with the poem's content, the poverty of our formal practice and imagination becomes quite shocking. Particularly when we contrast seven hundred forms to the two or three unconscious "free-form" closed forms most contemporary poets, particularly emerging poets, default to in their writing practice. Perhaps not surprisingly, a growing number of contemporary poets are now working in traditional closed forms. This re-encountering of closed forms may invigorate all our unthinking, habit-bound approaches to form.

If you are curious as to how to assess the appropriateness of form for each of your poems or prose texts, look for the following indications.

When form is not appropriate, your narratives are:

- Predictable; not surprising
- Resistant to being worked with
- Unclear in focus and intention
- Over-simplified
- Inaccurately paced, sequenced, proportioned
- Subject to being misread
- Lacking embodiment, the reader is not deeply located
- A slog to write

When form is appropriate:

- Your narratives surprise you, even frighten you
- You are fully present, embodied, keenly aware you are on the scent

- You have a conviction that the narrative in its own right is compelling
- You occupy a clear, authentic voice
- You trust the narrative and images to unfold of their own logic
- The form begins to collaborate with you, helping you generate the narrative
- Your narrative attracts and fully engages your reader
- It is easy and inviting to re-enter the narrative as you write and revise

Let's consider two examples. One memoir writer I worked with had recorded a number of remarkable, short exchanges between herself and her mother. The focus of the narrative was the final years of her mother's life and her mother's increasing dementia. Many of these recorded exchanges were gems — delightfully free from grammatical constraints, normal logic, and propriety. The intrinsic formal challenge here was to not be seduced by foregrounding these exchanges. The writer wanted to begin each chapter with one of them, but this prevented the reader from accessing an authentic experience of these exchanges. Why? Because they were anything but predictable: the memoirist never knew when they would happen, and, when they did, if they would be trying or poetic. The intrinsic form signalled that these delightful exchanges had to occur in a non-programmatic manner throughout the narrative.

For an example in poetry, see what you notice about how my understanding of intrinsic form evolved between the first draft (scored in a conventional open form) and the final draft in *only this blue*, which stands naked in its altered formal reality.

(Early draft)
I myself am an unknown season
a-rhythmical, differently balanced
with things cut out, off, things put in,
things thin-bare, tight and wane
stitched together, falling out
unspeakable sensations of never the same

(Final draft)
I myself am an unknown season
a-rhythmical
                , differently
balanced
with things cut out
                                and off
and
            things put in
things
            thin-bare,
            tight and
wane
things
stitched together
, falling out
unspeakable sensations of never the same

Territory and Landmarks

I've almost completed a solid draft, but the narrative's unfolding still seems murky. What might be causing this?

Even with inspiring subject matter and a skillful grasp of the techniques of craft, our narratives can still fall flat or flounder. To extricate oneself from this insufferable place, it is crucial to see the whole territory of the narrative. With longer narratives (novel, poetry or essay collection, novella, suite of poems, collection of short stories, long poem, or non-fiction manuscript), we can see only one page at a time. It's a bit like viewing a mountain range through a monocular field glass. Fortunately, there are methods for taking in the scope, shape, and patterns of the narrative.

One way I see the whole territory of a narrative is to spread its pages out as much as possible. If your narrative isn't too long, spread it out on a large floor or tape all its pages on the walls for a few days. If it is a book-size narrative, then I spread it out section by section or chapter by chapter and record what I discover with each portion as I go. What impression does it give you visually: solid as a wall, fractured, porous, static, chaotic, undulating? How does this visual experience of the materiality of your narrative relate to its content and spirit? I allow myself to move in a non-linear way around the narrative and zero in on spots, areas, or sections that excite me, unnerve me, irritate me, leave me indifferent or bored — spots that confuse, move, intrigue, depress, or delight me. I then assess or sense what is provoking these various responses, and this in turn gives me clues for what kind of revisions are called for. I stay with this process until no further insights or observations occur.

Another revealing way to check a narrative is to track its tangents. Tangents are areas where the narrative appears to swerve off topic or appears to linger too long on something that seems incidental or insignificant. Tangents, however, can be where one of the most compelling aspects of the narrative resides. This possibility is overlooked more often than creative writing teachers or books on creative writing acknowledge. So, pause and enter a state of curiosity before hitting the delete key. Consider what a tangent might be telling you. It may indeed be weakening the narrative, but it may also be attempting to signal you about some seemingly small but significant aspect of the narrative that needs to be foregrounded more. Read each tangent carefully — consider it with your whole body, and if it is particularly vexing test it out on a couple of your first readers.

If your narrative is short, such as a short prose piece or a suite of poems, follow the same procedure as in the previous exercise, but do it line by line/sentence by sentence and stanza by stanza/paragraph by paragraph. On the other hand, if your narrative is long, such as a novel or memoir, mix up the order or sequence: juxtapose them to jar yourself out of your perceptual gridlock. Also try pulling out sections — all one character's dialogue, all the scenes happening in secondary settings, all seemingly minor themes — and determine how well these coincide with the narrative's intentions.

When I find areas that do not coincide, it's most productive if I do not jump in to fix them but rather take the time needed to analyze in order to discover what they suggest. In my experience, I know that it is absolutely necessary to assemble these different narrative slices physically in different piles or areas. Providing them with their own discrete physical environments is crucial, because my body often knows what the narrative's body requires better than my planning, frustrated, invested mind.

Each narrative recognizes its territory: what's in it and what's not; what's foreground and what's background; what's beyond its scope or perspective. Once you also have recognized its territory, it becomes easier to delete that remarkable metaphor if it distracts from the poem; save that witty but out of place character for another narrative; delete that 25 percent of your novel's plodding commentary. All these forms of revision are part of the writing process; nothing is a waste of time.

Over the years, I have come to find that this stage of revision is as intriguing, and often as creative and surprising, as the inscription process itself.

When you feel resistance to making the changes the narrative requires ("But I worked for months on that section!"), take a deep breath, unpeel your white knuckles, and trust that the narrative is much more likely to thrive in the end.

Another effective method for analyzing the whole of your narrative is to look closely at how its landmarks or points of intensification are functioning, are signalling the manner in which the narrative is moving forward.

We can think of points of intensification as places where break-throughs, revelations, confrontations, integration, or transformations occur. These are usually plot-based, action and dialogue. I am speaking here of their more embedded forms:

- Repeated key words
- Evolving, related images
- Telling physical gestures

Points of intensification make a narrative embodied, evocative. They often signal a deeper meaning, or the accumulation of meaning through a building pattern. These are landmarks in the narrative. Sometimes we are aware of them — even look for them — though more often we notice them unthinkingly. They subconsciously guide us along when we are focused on more important things. Points of intensification are like intonations that cue the reader as to the exact meaning of what is being implied or said in the narrative. They typically, but not always, happen throughout the narrative in some of the following configurations:

- Clustered at different points in the narrative
- In counterpoint to the movement of the narrative's storyline
- Frontloaded and functioning like a radar of what's to come
- Resisting the flow of the narrative periodically as a way to signal its outcome is not what it appears it will be

Curiously, I cannot recall a writer ever lingering too long on a point of intensification required by the narrative. By far the most common fault is not to recognize or trust these points of intensity and to render them in a superficial manner. As writers, we know when we have resisted strip-mining quickly across the surface and dropped down to pit-mine a point of intensification. We know, because suddenly we find ourselves sitting on the edges of our chairs as we track the surprising places the narrative needs to go. We have a sense of collaborating, not corralling. Points of intensification are, in fact, what often compel us to write. They are unexplored terrain — and they change us.

So why do we resist points of intensification so much? Are we afraid of boring our readers? Are we still in the trance of a coma story? I suspect the more common reason is our mistaken perception that a good writer is in control of his material. True mastery is the willingness to face the unknown when we write. Relentlessly. Unflinchingly. Waiting patiently for the narrative to unveil itself. Even though we may have the necessary skills, vision, and experience as a writer — the narrative is always the one in charge.

In-fluencies # 5

The pleasures and skillfulness of storytelling resided with my mother and her sisters. On the heels of dessert, over coffee, they would entertain us with a repertoire of stories from their childhood and young adulthood. Some stories were nostalgic, some poignant, but most were humorous. My cousins and I never tired of them being told and retold.

Although all five sisters volleyed for centre stage and interrupted one another with their own versions, one sister was clearly the most compelling storyteller. She had a flawless sense of timing, nuance, and irony.

In my mid-twenties, I discovered that this aunt was also an avid reader who read into her early nineties. And, I also discovered something else. One day while walking with my dad, I puzzled out loud over an incongruence I saw in this aunt: bitterness. There seemed to be nothing in her life that would be provoking this, yet every so often it flashed like sunlight off a car's rear-view mirror. I was stunned by my father's reply: "Bob had other women." Our conversation crashed to a halt.

It was from her that I learned the alchemy of narrative.

Unpublished prose, by Betsy Warland, 2008.

The Computer

What do I need to consider when writing on the computer?

The computer is enigma. It is efficient, intelligent, yet highly susceptible to sudden chaos and error; a prototype for material and conceptual activity. The computer, like Narcissus's reflection, resembles us far more than any other material with which we work. Yet, as Narcissus discovered, it is not us. The computer is our private secretary, research assistant, personal librarian, friendly bookseller, Xerox person, copy editor, layout designer, typesetter, post office, and courier. As the computer provides us with a professional in-house staff, it depopulates our lives of the array of personalities with whom we used to interact within our community. Simultaneously, the computer has made our lives so porous as to almost eliminate the distinction between public and private activity.

Everything interfaces with everything.

Everything interrupts everything: retreating from the non-stop doing and techno-communicating world is becoming more and more difficult. As writers — for whom concentrated, solitary writing and reflecting time is a necessity — this is of particular concern. I both appreciate and am ambivalent toward my collaborative relationship with my computer, in part because of the seeming similarity of consciousness. A summation of my history with computer is in order.

I wrote my first book prior to the advent of privately owned word processors. I fell in love with my typewriter during my first decade as a poet in much the same way as recent generations of young writers fall in love with their first computers. By the time I was writing my second book, a few writers had begun to switch from typewriters to PCs. During those early years, writers frequently lost portions (and sometimes the whole) of manuscripts due to their nascent computer skills and naive neglect in not printing hard copies. To have one's entire manuscript vanish as a result of pushing, or not pushing, the right button was a terrifying thought. Despite this, I began to consider buying a computer while working on my third manuscript, *serpent (w)rite*. This was a complex manuscript requiring endless cutting, rearranging, pasting, revising, and retyping. On a computer, these procedures could be easily accomplished.

At this time, I also noticed that after a year or two of other writers using computers, meticulous, established authors were publishing their work prematurely. This phenomenon was puzzling at first. Gradually it became apparent that their previous sharp eye had been fooled by the finished look the computer screen and printout provided. The impression of a piece of writing looking finished when it is not continues to fool writers, particularly emerging writers. As a professional writer who has worked on computer for a few decades now, I have become more able to identify when I have been seduced by this sleight of sight problem and always review and revise my texts in hard copy. It is a phenomenon, regardless of how long we have been writing, for which we must remain alert.

I found that I was still reluctant to abandon my intimacies with my typewriter. I loved my typewriter's physicality; I loved cleaning it and changing its ribbons. I loved its sounds and smells. I enjoyed the repetitive gesture of returning the carriage and the simple and visible mechanics of it reminiscent of my favourite instrument — the piano. I was intrigued and comforted by how the same model of typewriter gradually responded to each writer's distinct patterns of finger pressure on its keys — how the print quality of the character *a* could signal which friend's writing I was reading. Midway through my fifth manuscript (a collection of essays), logic prevailed, and I made the switch. This computer, in fact, began my sixth manuscript — a book I had not intended to write.

When booting up my new computer in 1991, it always reported "o characters." Repeatedly seeing this phrase in a white font against a black screen seemed a metaphoric reminder of the memory loss I had recently navigated my way through — regarding an abusive relationship — and that phrase became the genesis of *The Bat Had Blue Eyes*. My computer clearly became my collaborator. It seemed to insist on my writing the narrative I had refused to write. That simple phrase of zero characters integrated autobiographical-based narrative, language-centred writing, and spiritual practice for me for the first time in my writing life. They met on the page as they never had.

As with any new, complex relationship, I had to learn how and when to engage, and not engage, with my computer. Initially, I continued to inscribe first drafts by hand then transfer them onto a disc for revisions. Efficiency — the great temptation — soon convinced me to inscribe first drafts directly on the computer. Over time, however, efficiency proved not to be the best criterion; it was eroding many of my inscription methods that I knew to be of value. I noticed that my inscribing on the computer made me less willing to allow myself the crucial pausing and musing times required for sensing the narrative's needs. I found myself missing the almost tactile record of revision tracks left on the page with pencil. I noted that my hard-won critical capacities were not as acute and reliable when I proofed and edited on screen. I continue to find this to be true — it is as though one angle of assessment is missing.

Often, I felt too confined by inscribing in one environment, my office. Gradually, I once again began to follow the erratic methods and rhythms of inscription necessitated by each narrative's sensibilities. My ninth book, *Bloodroot*, pushed me away from the computer during its initial inscription; it pushed me out of my office and into my living room, a place I had never inscribed in. *Bloodroot* required a different embodiment from me during inscription. Insisted on a domestic, intimate environment conducive to extended periods of waiting and reflecting between segments of inscription: it insisted upon close proximity, and I wrote and revised it (up to fifteen drafts per piece) in longhand on the folder my father had given me decades prior, on my lap.

As writers, we need to question what adjustments in our habits of inscription each narrative might require. One novelist I worked with was troubled by her resistance to writing on the computer after her daytime word processing job, but made herself write on it, all the while interpreting her resistance as indicative of inadequacies in the narrative, of her inabilities as a writer, or, on a bad day, both. It was a revelation to her when I suggested that she shift to another mode of inscription — that she allow herself to do this routinely until her novelist self felt eager to work at her computer. It is useful to keep in mind that the computer not only processes our narratives — we are also processed by the computer's language, hidden narratives, and predetermined logic.

Marshall McLuhan suggested that the computer is an extension of our bodies, and that it can flatten out the complexities and subtleties of our human exchange. This flattening out has proven to sometimes encourage a disassociation that can become so profound as to disconnect us from the real repercussions of our actions. Serious misunderstandings that erupt via email exchanges are a common example.

The computer is enigma, a paradox.

The lineage of the computer is very different from that of the typewriter. The typewriter evolved from the printing press: its roots are literature and religion. The computer's lineage, *com-, together + putare, to settle (an account)* , is one of mathematical calculation used in the manufacturing of wartime aircraft, and the crucial cracking of the Nazi Enigma machine code by the British Intelligence Colossus machine, considered to be the first computer.

The computer, by design, knows its mind. On this we depend. The logic, however, of the narrative's lines and our narrating mind must always be a flexible logic. A logic that redefines itself with each narrative we write. Ultimately, on this we must depend.

The Writing Room

Might where I write affect how and what I write?

A writer recalls each writing room with an intimacy that rivals the recollection of each lover. As with lovers, the suitability of each room varies, but the devotion is the same — we fall in love again and again — and though physical attraction is pivotal, it is the rare experience of being held comfortably in the timelessness of the act of writing — as in a lover's arms — that we are most drawn to.

Unlike most art forms, writing requires periods of unremitting, solitary concentration. Having been a visual artist as well as a writer into my late twenties, I know that the porosity of making visual art is far greater than that of writing. People walk in and out of your painting studio, converse, comment on your piece, watch it evolve. This kind of active companionship among visual artists in their studios would cause most of us writers to completely lose our line of thought or throw us off the scent while in hot pursuit of our narratives. As writers, we tend to be more cautious, reluctant to talk about our work in the midst of writing — to the point of superstition.

Our creative process is more akin to composers' creative processes. Listening is our generative source.

Writing, like music, is everywhere in our daily lives. Conversely, production of our writing remains invisible. Publishers do not make studio visits. Photographers rarely shoot photographs of writers at work.

Due to our contemporary writing practice of inscribing on the computer, as well as researching, reading, and posting on the web, the need for a writing room set apart may be more urgent than ever before. Our devotion to language and narrative is of a different nature than our relationship to language and narrative in the world outside our writing rooms. We must do everything within our power to nourish and invigorate this devotion, for, in truth, everything in daily living conspires against this kind of concentration and reverence.

Accessing a writing environment, both privately and publicly, is not only a challenge in our time. A century ago, in her groundbreaking book, *A Room of One's Own*, Virginia Woolf persuasively argued that women writers were undermined not only by the lack of a writing room of their own but also by the exclusion of women from centres of higher education and their respective libraries.[1] Would Woolf have written her books without having had a room of her own along with the benefits of her personal library?

For each writer, a room must possess certain basic qualities. For me these are: surrounding quiet, ample natural light, a door that closes, a window that opens and that I enjoy looking out of, agreeable colours on the walls and floors, and a layout that allows for quirkiness — I prefer my writing table placed at an angle in a room.

The room must hold my collaborators comfortably. My desk, reading chair, equipment and supplies, desk and floor lamps, books and bookshelves, files and file cabinet, cup, talismans, visual art, and dictionary stand must occupy the space efficiently and imaginatively. In our mutual compatibility, my writing room helps sustain the narrative pulse of my various writing projects, and I enter into my narratives as eagerly as I step into my room.

---

1. Virginia Woolf, *A Room of One's Own* (Harmondsworth, Middlesex: Penguin Books Ltd., 1974).

breathing

I have had a writing room about as often as I have not had one. Economic constraints necessitate our being flexible as writers. Often we must improvise. If you have no writing room, it is crucial to:

- Identify the periods of the day or night when you write best and maintain these as much as possible
- With the above in mind, fit your writing time into the existing rhythms of those around you (bedroom during the day, quiet café at night, etc.)
- Close the door of your attention to all other distractions and demands (use good quality earplugs, and avoid distractions)
- Protect your writing room within yourself so that your solitary place of concentration and creative energy is not dependent upon an ideal writing room

I have worked in corners of bedrooms, corners of living rooms, nooks, hotel rooms, libraries, shared office spaces, libraries, and quiet cafés. Crucial to the success of these spaces were the rhythms of others sharing these spaces — their patterns of activities did not conflict with my own. Some writers fare well in shared spaces (Jane Austen in her kitchen) and some do not (Virginia Woolf). This depends on personality and also on the nature of your writing. Does it require acute attention, or is it amenable to bouncing off what's around it? A few writers I know inscribe in their minds and write it in a notebook while commuting to their jobs in their car, or on public transit.

Sometimes what the narrative requires is to not inscribe in a writing room. When I began writing *Bloodroot: Tracing the Untelling of Motherloss*, that narrative literally pulled me out of my writing room — away from my computer — into my living room. Soon I understood that the nature of that particular narrative required my inscribing it in a domestic space by longhand in a folder that my father had given me years prior to my mother's death.

A writing room is the one site writing fully occupies.

Our writing *room, rewe-, to open; space*, whether actual, shared, or portable, is where we open into the ever-inviting, endless horizon of the page.

Quote-tidian # 4

Fernanda Viveiros: And, finally, do you have some last words of advice on the most important steps in developing as a writer?

Betsy Warland: Write the narratives that hunt you down: the ones that surprise and terrify you, the very ones that you often would have preferred not to write! Take risks in content and form. Wake up to your habits of craft and ways of working with narrative and relentlessly question the suitability of using them with each narrative you write. Accept that each narrative has its own specific requirements and that what you brilliantly figured out for your previous narrative often does not suit the ones that follow. Accept that nearly every narrative you write will require far more work and far more time to fully realize than you ever imagined. Leonard Cohen usually takes a minimum of a year to write one song. Read voraciously. Find companionship; seek out and build community for yourself. Give readings as much as possible for this gives you a concrete sense of where revisions are still needed as well as where your audience responds positively to your narrative. Accept that you will often feel "discouraged." Put your trust in the act of writing itself: the timelessness of it; the endless intrigue of it; the rigorousness of it; and how this nourishes you because everything else about your life as a writer is secondary (at best) in comparison.

"Betsy Warland: Building a Community of Writers," *Word Works*, Fall 2006.

Sustaining Yourself as a Writer

Sometimes I am overwhelmed, discouraged. What will help me persist and grow as a writer?

I.

How do you sustain yourself as a writer? Perhaps surprisingly, this becomes a pivotal question the longer you write and the more you publish. In a word: tenacity. Sheer tenacity. *Sheer*, meaning from the state of *mere* to almost nothingness, so that we do not get in the way of each narrative's specific requirements. *Tenacity*, referring to the state of irreducible devotion to the act of writing itself.

> Between the page and the writer is a magnetism more compelling than any other relationship.[1]

Sheer. Thin. To learn to navigate lack. Lack of writing time, which usually is synonymous with lack of money to enable writing time. Lack of understanding what this narrative needs. Lack of faith in one's self as a writer. Lack of writing companions. Lack of support from our intimates. Lack of interest from publishers. Lack of reviews when published. Lack of professional support in the form of writing grants and invitations to professional events. Lack of finding your book on bookstore and library shelves. Lack of almost any financial gain comparable to the time invested in writing, polishing, finding a publisher, and promoting your book.

To learn to sheer off, deviate from, sidestep lack — inventively, objectively, flagrantly — is to make lack a generative, fortifying source.

---

1. Betsy Warland, *Breathing the Page*, "The Page," 2010.

You might be thinking that this sounds rather bleak. Or you may be thinking, "What about talent? It's inspiration and our innate talent that keeps us going." Yes, but I suggest that this is merely the match that strikes the narrative's flame. Tenacity, however, is what feeds the fire until the narrative is fully realized. Published. Read.

II.

The key to sustaining ourselves as writers is this: we must take care of our needs as writers ourselves. Although this may seem obvious, it isn't. The hope creeps in periodically that others will support us in meeting our deadlines, will understand and always respect our writing time, will contribute to our financial circumstances in various ways to enable our writing. Sometimes there are residencies, grants, retreats, and the rare bestselling book, but most of the time no one will enable the conditions for us to write and publish. It is up to us. Each time we renew this resolve, our other skills for sustaining ourselves take firmer hold. If these self-sustaining abilities are insufficient, publishing is a moot point. When we have honed these abilities and finished a publishable manuscript, an entirely different set of skills must kick in to sustain us through the often arduous process of finding an appropriate publisher, negotiating a contract, perhaps consulting an intellectual properties lawyer about libel or defamation, working with the press's editor on final revisions, proofreading the galleys, promoting the book, and fielding the unpredictable critical reactions.

III.

A writer can often feel that everything conspires against the act of writing. As a profession, for the majority of us it is an illogical pursuit, offering little financial reward and uncertain reception once we have published a manuscript. Yet many people dream of becoming a writer — more than they do about any other creative occupation — believing that they have a book in them. As an art form, writing is by far the closest to our ordinary, daily lives — revolving around print, storytelling, computers, longhand jottings, paper, tables and chairs. Because writing is so ordinary and does not require extra equipment, special materials, or — some think — space, it is assumed that we can simply add writing on to the rest of our lives. Writing is considered to be an activity that bears frequent interruption, for in daily life it usually is a porous activity. As writers, however, we are endlessly having to set and reset parameters for protecting our concentrated writing time with our intimates and others around us, as well as with ourselves, and even with our writer-friends. When writing or preparing to write, there is no interruption that "will only take a few moments," for on the heels of that interruption we lose the focus and momentum of what we were in the midst of, and it can take hours, even days, to re-find it.

The fact that few writers are able to afford a writing room — that we most often write in multi-purpose spaces — compounds the likelihood of disruption of focus. Recognizing your least contested islands of concentrated writing time is crucial. Some writers do their thinking about their writing projects, pursue research, take notes, and even do inscription during their routine transit time. Some rise an hour or two before their intimates and write, or, conversely, write after everyone is asleep. Some go once or twice a year to writing retreats and write flat-out, accomplishing a remarkable amount within a short span of time. Others write in quiet cafés or libraries. Some, like myself, set aside a couple of half-days or a day a week — a time that has the fewest conflicting demands — to write. An advantage of our art form is its portability; it allows for a variety of inscription sites.

Identifying the time of the day, evening, week, even season during which our creative and concentration abilities are typically at their optimum is also crucial. For me, the best time is mornings into mid-afternoon. But once again, our firm resolve to tell everyone we are unavailable and not to be interrupted must also be applied to ourselves. Bifurcating activities such as answering phone calls, reviewing our to-do lists, checking voice mail, email, text messages, postal mail, and calendars, or engaging in any seemingly simple problem-solving inevitably derail us and must be resisted.

As writers, we must learn to be profoundly self-responsible. There is no one else who will take care of our practical needs as a writer or do our time management for us. Writing is often said to be the most solitary of the art forms; correspondingly, nearly everything in our writing life depends on one thing: ourselves.

IV.

I do not recall ever having heard a writer say that he has too much time to write. There is never enough time to write. This is our chronic complaint. To be fair, it is also a fact, and, not infrequently, a tormenting one. Occasionally, I hear emerging writers bemoan not being able to write during a period of time that they had set aside to write full-time. Their inability to write, however, is more about their self-doubts and nascent discipline than it is about time; more about the illusion that if we had all the time we wanted, our writing would flourish. But it isn't time that does the writing.

I have come to believe that we writers have a particular, perhaps even peculiar, relationship with time. That our relationship to time may be the basis of our bond with each other as much as is our fascination with narrative itself. When I have given myself over in deep surrender to the act of writing, I am outside of time — time becomes an amorphous, energetic substance — and it is then that I glimpse eternity. The grip and pressures of linear time are released: minutes can seem to be hours; hours seem minutes; and the malleability, even benevolence, of time is utterly elating. Other writers may experience this somewhat differently, but it is another almost unspoken reason why we are preoccupied with time. It is in this timeless, transformative state that we are able to access other historical and imaginative times from which our narratives emit, or by which they are influenced, for we are then unencumbered by the constraints and prevailing logic of the real time we purportedly live in.

As writers, we also become adept at occupying different times simultaneously, conflating disparate times that are related associatively. Additionally, we move in and out of the time frames and sensibilities of our narrative each time we work on it, each time we set it aside until returning to work on it again. Occasionally, we also put a portion of or our entire manuscript in a drawer for a while to gain perspective on it. With the passage of linear time, we return to it with a more objective eye. All these relationships with time can puzzle and frustrate people who are not writers. Recently, an emerging writer told me about a conversation with her teenage daughter, who inquired, "So, Mom, how many more hours before you finish your manuscript?" This perfectly logical question is illogical when it comes to writing. Even we ourselves can be baffled by our encounters with writing and narrative time. It is not unusual for us to think that we have finished a manuscript several times before we actually have.

Given that writers typically have jobs and familial and intimate commitments, as well as having practical and professional tasks to attend to in our writing lives, we actually occupy the timeless state of inscription during a minority of our waking hours. It is imperative that we find an array of strategies to keep the door ajar on the narratives we are writing. Our methodology is not as important as is our devotion, our resolve. During these not-writing phases, I jot down notes, undertake additional research, pay attention to my ideas, dreams, and reoccurring images, words, and surprising synchronicities. I eavesdrop, read, watch, attend whatever feeds my relationship to the narrative, and consider structural alternatives while standing in a lineup.

When we are approaching the threshold back into our narrative, various kinds of meditative movements and simple repetitive activities — like sweeping or taking a walk — assist us to cross over the threshold with more ease. Not infrequently, this approaching the threshold time can appear to be procrastination. Undoubtedly, sometimes it is. But more often, I believe, it is not. Yes, it may appear to be avoidance or aimlessness, but always assess if this is, in fact, the case, for crucial preparatory time may be undermined by your harsh, misguided self-criticism. It is as important for us to protect this kind of time as it is to protect our writing time. I have come to recognize that preparatory activities in my brain and sensations in my body are quite specific — almost like a gravitational shift occurring. As a dog conflates its pre-domesticated genetic memory of beating down the grass in the wild with its domesticated ritual of circling before it lies down, I typically must circle my narrative numerous times.

V.

The seductive, romantic image of the writer in his garret, his time his own, is just that. Historically, there were some authors who were masters of their days, but not as many as we might think. Those who were were independently wealthy or supported by a relative or spouse. Yet, support can be double-edged: Colette's husband locked her in her writing room to ensure that she wrote, but also to ensure their livelihood! There have been periods in history when it was more possible to make a living as an author than it is today. Few contemporary authors can write full-time. As writers, we essentially have two choices. One is to hold a job or have a profession that has built-in spaces for writing, such as working as a food server with flexible shift work — if you are a morning writer, you write then and work evenings — or working as a teacher, with several extended paid leaves during which you are able to write. The advantage of this option is that you can be certain and confident of when you will have your writing times, and if you learn to pace yourself — do all the preparatory research and thinking about structural concerns between these predetermined writing times — you can be ready to dive in.

The second option is to develop a set of writing-related skills and become a freelancer. These related skills include editing; working in a bookstore, a publishing house, or a library; being a translator; doing independent journalism or technical writing; teaching creative writing or literature; being a manuscript consultant; creating a popular blog; etc. The advantage of this option is that when you are not able to do your own manuscript writing, you are still being stimulated, you continue to thrive within the sensibilities of the writing and literary communities.

As writers, we commit ourselves to a life of modest, even uncertain, means. Many of us live close to the poverty line. This hit me hard a few decades ago when I had the opportunity to house-sit for a respected senior poet. Her place was a rental; she couldn't afford to own. It was a large, renovated chicken coop. Her sparse belongings resembled those of a grad student.

Few of us are affluent authors living off advances and royalties from bestsellers. If an author's books are not routinely on academic course lists nor of interest to the commercial market's trends, royalties provide a partial income at best. Increasingly, writers are self-publishing via their own websites and blogs. As a writer builds readership, a sizeable income can be made via sales of their books, chapbooks, CDs, and speaking, teaching, consulting, and mentoring services.

In a recent conversation with a Toronto creative non-fiction writer, we discovered that we had both come to the realization that we have been essentially giving our work away. More and more writers are seeking reversion of rights from their publishers, buying up their warehoused stock, and selling their books from their own websites. Self-publishing has also made a respectable comeback.

The challenges of earning a living that sustains us are not so dissimilar to the challenges of writing. Sometimes it is possible to pursue them both as creative acts. I have had periods ranging from full-time writing to absolutely no writing time. Although we can understandably long for a period of full-time writing, we can't afford to pine too much for this. Over the past decade, due to life circumstances, I have developed a viable freelance writing related career and have learned how to write in punctuated periods of writing time. This is when I discovered how to keep the door ajar, recognized how to foster my circling, preparatory time, and developed the ability to write with deep focus for much shorter periods of time. In some respects, these skills have made me a better writer. Wishing it different can be counterproductive, can even lead to writer's block. It is essential for us to be inventive, tenacious, wily.

VI.

Writers need the companionship of other writers, but how do you find other writers? This is not a rhetorical question. Contrasted to other artists, writers are more difficult to identify. Other art forms often involve collaborative activities at various stages, whereas writers remain solitary and self-reliant (with the exception of working on scripts) throughout nearly every aspect of our writing lives. The manner in which specific body types, gestures, choice of clothing, and accompanying tools of the trade signal actors, dancers, visual artists, musicians, and composers in public does not apply to writers. Nine people intently writing on computers or by longhand in a café may be writers. But, just as likely, none of them is.

I have a vivid recollection of when I first realized just how unidentifiable we are. I was teaching my first ten-day residential writing school. As people arrived — sporadically, lugging suitcases and writing gear — I occasionally passed them in the dark, narrow hallways and our voices would reach out to one another with a tentative "Hello." That evening there was a faculty and student orientation. As I walked into the room, I wondered if another interest group was also at the retreat centre, for this appeared to be the wrong group of people. No one remotely looked like a writer. Then I spotted another faculty member I knew, waved hello, and took a seat. I continued to feign nonchalant glances around, asking myself, "Are these writers?" They looked like people I would pass by in a supermarket.

After a few days of engaging with the thinking and work of my students, I easily saw the writer in each of them. Ever since, I have been intrigued by just how incognito we are. Although this makes it easier for us to observe, eavesdrop, gather material, do research without being questioned, at the same time it makes it harder for us to recognize one another and meet. Unlike other artists, we do not routinely co-occupy rehearsal space or shared studio, performance, or exhibition sites. The spaces in which we meet are periodic and brief — such as a reading or a conference — or closed membership sites, such as an MFA creative writing degree.

The informal, writer-instigated gatherings to talk writing that existed in the past — Thursday nights at a certain pub, frequent dinner parties when a visiting author came to town — have almost vanished. Local literary communities have become more diverse, fragmented. Few writers seem to have the time to organize such gatherings. More and more, these exchanges and relationships are virtual ones online.

This is likely one of the reasons that educational opportunities for emerging writers have expanded: courses, workshops, retreats, creative writing programs have become the only reliable venues for emerging writers to meet their peers and access the training and support they need from established writers. Yes, there are some valid concerns about possible institutionalization of emerging writers: graduates being strong on craft but two-dimensional in terms of content; a homogeneity of style; access to the literary community being determined by who can afford tuition; and grants, awards, and publication becoming more institutional-affiliate influenced — but what are the viable alternatives? And, if we are honest with ourselves, a number of these dynamics were happening prior to the flourishing of education-based writers' training. Contrasted to when I grew up as a young writer, emerging writers today are also more confused about questions of structure and focus. I suspect this reflects the profound destabilization of narrative we are collectively experiencing in every aspect of our lives. In contrast to a couple of decades ago and in light of all these changes, emerging writers today need more guidance and support. I do see remarkable growth in many emerging writers who have had these kinds of support and training.

VII.

There are, of course, additional ways to find companionship as writers. Satisfying companionship can be found in such activities as attending literary events, giving and organizing readings, writing reviews, volunteering at an event or for a journal, joining writers' organizations, sitting on literary juries, participating in peer-led writing workshops, submitting to journals and competitions, establishing an online presence, and apprenticing with an established author who is teaching creative writing.

Some of our most cherished companions may be dead ones: authors whose books, thinking, and passions profoundly speak to and inspire us. Urge us on. Embody a sense of home ground we can access at will. Some of our companions will be contemporary writers with whom we share obvious connections of background, lived experience, writing styles, preoccupations, and pursuit of a set of particular ideas. We may meet some of these authors through their publications, and they may become personal friends. Writers who are dissimilar to us, whose writing provokes, disturbs, and invigorates us, are equally important companions. Here, the vast world of print offers unlimited access through blogs and new media, publishing on the web, books in translation, and international writers reading at festivals.

Companionship can also happen in surprising ways. Nearly three decades ago, I attended a reading given by a francophone author. Although my knowledge of French was almost nil, I found this author's reading to be riveting. How can this be? She so deeply embodied the shifting emotional states, the distinct sculptural sounding of the narrator's voice, and the resonant structure of her narrative that her reading and writing were one. This created a remarkable focus within her, and within her audience. The power of the writing was unleashed. I had been groping towards this in my own readings, but had never before encountered it so completely. Three decades later, that reading and author still companion me.

Not infrequently, people who have attended one of my readings tell me that I am courageous. This comment never ceases to surprise me. I believe we literary writers write out of necessity. I believe that our narratives hunt us down; haunt us until we write them; even ambush us when we try to write something else in an attempt to escape them. It is only much later, when giving a reading or publishing our work, that perhaps courage enters in, particularly if our narrative is one to which readers are likely to have an initial resistance. Many of my narratives fall into this category. Fortunately, these are also the narratives — once we can access an audience — that can move and invigorate readers the most. It is paramount to remember that it is the writing itself that is giving the reading (not our persona). As we read word by word, we become the narrative's single-focused, primary listener. The encounter is between the narrative and its listeners. During this encounter, I can also listen through my "third ear," particularly when reading works-in-progress. This is a crucial part of my writing process. As I read, I can hear where I have erred from the veracity, tone, and flow of the narrative and where I have been faithful to it. It is almost magical. For me, this is an axis of companionship where all forces meet: it is one of the companionships I cherish the most.

The writing community is a small community not that different from any small community. Frankly, it took me some years to understand this because we are a community that idealizes itself. A proudly held tenet within our community is that we are judged and supported on the excellence of our work alone. I took this to be absolute truth when I was an emerging writer. I was deeply impressed by this high-mindedness. I now know this admirable tenet is only erratically realized. Literary history confirms this. A

breathing

significant number of great books around the world were rejected as many as a hundred times by publishers — came perilously close to never seeing the light of day — before a publisher finally offered the author a contract. Amplifying this phenomenon is the corporatization of the publishing and book selling industries, which is resulting in marketing making the decisions more and more often than the publisher deciding on the merit of the manuscript or book. Indeed, there are other decisive criteria — usually unspoken in public — that determine which writers are frequently, even automatically, included. By inclusion, I am thinking of everything from being anthologized to getting grants, reviews, festival invitations, and awards. It is important to acknowledge this reality: our writing can indeed achieve excellence and still not be supported.

Like any small community, we are reluctant to forgive perceived wrongs and aberrant ways. I caution emerging writers to think through their actions and comments very carefully, to be prepared to live with them, for they may have repercussions for a long time. Sometimes self-interests collide and everyone suffers in one way or another — I can attest to this. Vexing or offending someone from time to time is unavoidable; however, whatever we can do to stay on good terms is important, for few of us have an excess of support!

Ultimately, our most crucial and reliable companion — the one that sustains and incites us — is the act of writing itself.

VIII.

Over and over we seek out intimate companionship with each narrative we write. We fall in love, or sometimes in hate, which ends up being the same thing. We are given our narrative material; it entrusts itself into our hands. Initially, it may seem that we are drawn to it, that we choose it. Or sometimes, it may seem that the narrative material is seeking us out. Occasionally there is mutual, simultaneous attraction. But more often, in the early stages, we must elbow our way through our resistances and avoidances until we accept our narrative. Then a pact is made, and we and our narrative are in it together. Once we commit to the narrative material that hunts us down, it will prove to be the narrative that pushes us the hardest to learn more about craft, more about the human condition, more about the possibilities of perception.

When our narrative becomes our companion, the forcefulness of the insistent narrative sustains us through debilitating doubt. Then, when we have finished the narrative, that same force will fuel us to find a publisher so that our readers, too, can encounter this narrative's particular force. What the writer and the publisher then must share is the fact that they are both drawn to the narrative; they must eagerly give their allegiance to it. True, the publisher must be more concerned with producing and selling the book, but a book stands a better chance of selling well if the publisher takes pleasure in it.

How then to determine who the ideal publisher is? This in itself is a kind of narrative pursuit: What will the story of our search for a publisher be? Who will be the characters? What will the backstory be? Given that nearly all publishing houses and literary journals are sorely understaffed, more responsibilities are falling on writers. Thus, when we submit a manuscript, it must be as close as possible to a professionally edited clean manuscript. Nearly print-ready. This helps a publisher make an accurate assessment of how much editorial work the press will need to offer — which may well sway a decision to offer a contract or not.

As writers, we must also do market research and be able to speak knowledgeably about what other books are similar to, yet different from, ours, how positively they were reviewed, and how well they sold. We must be able to write a professional, curiosity-provoking, succinct manuscript précis and cover letter. Only then are we in a position to research specific publishers, study their backlist, talk to other authors who have published with them, study their website for for submission guidelines (do they want to see your entire manuscript, or only an initial summary?) and procedures (are they comfortable with multiple submissions or not?), and, if it seems a good match, send off a professionally formatted manuscript. Publishers are relying more on author-referred manuscripts versus unsolicited manuscripts. If you have worked in-depth with an author on your manuscript, inquire if that author feels your manuscript is ready and is of enough merit for that author to recommend it to a publisher. Then, wait. And wait. And wait. And when you receive the most frequent reply, "Sorry, this doesn't fit our list," begin again. Sometimes this takes months; more often it takes years. Finding a publisher can take longer than it took you to write the book! Tenacity? Tenacity in spades.

High-profile authors are often asked to submit their manuscripts to mainstream publishers. For some other authors, once you have published with a press, the publishing contract will have optioned your next book, or the publisher may simply be interested in publishing your subsequent book(s). But most authors must go through the arduous submitting process. Occasionally, a manuscript is snapped up because it fits a popular trend, addresses a socio-political hot topic, has the "I discovered this astonishing first-time author" marketing potential, is on a solid selling topic (like hockey, in Canada), or is recommended by an author who knows you and publishes with the publishing house you are approaching. These scenarios, however enticing, are not as frequent as we might imagine.

Here it is worth mentioning other or parallel alternatives to consider: self-publish a chapbook; publish excerpts from your manuscript in journals, magazines, zines, or on your blog or website; investigate self-publishing either in book form or online as an e-book or print-on-demand.

My decision to post this entire essay as a free pdf download on my website has proven to be a positive and productive experience. It has been empowering to publish the essay myself given the number of years it took to find the right publisher for *Breathing the Page*. I wish an essay such as this one had been available to me earlier on in my career; I wanted to make it easy to obtain by any writer who wanted it, so I decided to give it away. Since I posted it in September 2009, I have been amazed by how many writers and authors are reading and relishing it across the country. For some, this essay will be all they want; for others, they will want to read more and will buy the book.

Undoubtedly, we will see more and more writers and authors publishing and selling their work online. The benefits of having control over publication and, in some cases, significantly increasing your earnings from your publications are attractive. The possibility of reaching a much larger readership is also attractive. In my opinion, some manuscripts and writing are more suited for new media (all forms of electronic publishing options). Given the nature and style of my current work-in-progress, "Oscar of Between," I am planning to publish it in sequel form on my website.

breathing

In contrast, the nature of *Breathing the Page* suits a print-based book. Here's why. I already have evidence that it will appeal to teachers of creative writing and will be included on course lists. More significant, however, is that the entire book is written to be a steady companion to writers who will seek it out (read and re-read it) from time to time. I myself have numerous companion books on my shelves, and the very sight of their spines is enough to support an ongoing writing environment for me to work in. These companion books also serve a practical function: when teaching and doing manuscript consults, I can find examples of writing styles or appropriate publishers to approach in an associative, lateral manner that is not possible on the web. Regardless of how these changes in publishing unfold, one thing has not and will not change: it still takes a long time to write a strong, compelling manuscript.

Given how much work and effort is required on our part, and that publishers are overwhelmed with substandard, unsuitable submissions, the more skill we bring to finding the right publisher companion, the better the outcome.

Perhaps you may want to pause at this point to consider doing the concentric circles exercise that I created years ago. The value of this exercise is that at any given time — and it is instructive to do it from time to time — it precisely delineates what aspects of our writing lives are working well and what aspects are frustrating us. Most important are the first and inner circles: "How do I feel when I am immersed in writing?" and "How do I feel about the act, or process, of writing?" This is the core: what we must protect and nourish above all else. We must not allow other closely related, sometimes disheartening, concerns such as

"How do I feel about myself as a writer?" or "How do I feel about publishing my work?" to seep in and blur our feelings about how we feel when immersed in writing itself.

Think of the Concentric Circles of Writing Life as a cross-section of a tree with the centre circle representing the heartwood, or perhaps as water rippling out from the centre when a stone is dropped into it. Working outward from the centre circle, respond in a few words to the questions below. It is most revealing if you respond quickly rather than pondering your reply.

Circle 1 — How do I feel when I am immersed in writing?

Circle 2 — How do I feel about the act, or process, of writing?

Circle 3 — How do I feel about myself as a writer?

Circle 4 — How do I feel about my skills as a writer?

Circle 5 — How do I feel about my resources (equipment, place I write, time, editing help)?

Circle 6 — How do I feel about how those closest to me respond to my writing; me as a writer?

Circle 7 — How do I feel about the support and companionship I have from other writers?

Circle 8 — How do I feel about publishing my work?

Circle 9 — How do I feel about the reception of my work once it is published?

Now assess your diagram overall. Are there surprises? Are your responses consistent throughout, or do they vary considerably? Is there an area where your frustrations or uncertainties are all located? Once you have reviewed your diagram, consider ways

breathing

you can draw upon the areas in which you feel strong to give you confidence to address the areas that you need to change. These changes may be concrete, such as buying an ergonomically comfortable chair. Or these changes may be conceptual, such as shifting your perceptions from an aversion to promoting your book to seeing it as more similar to what motivates you to write: your desire to enable your narrative to reach its readers.

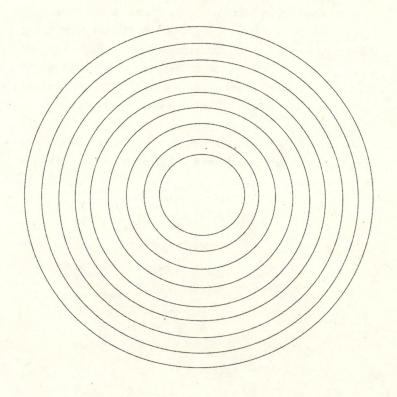

IX.

How can you most effectively sustain yourself as a writer? The source of renewal is the act of writing itself. It is the endless fascination with discovering each narrative's requirement: giving yourself over to each narrative's idiosyncratic force. All the other aspects of our writing and professional lives are important but provisional, unpredictable, transitory, even compromised.

In the act of writing I encounter the profoundest of teachers. This also extends to my experiences of teaching creative writing and doing manuscript development and editing. I am endlessly intrigued and challenged. It seems absolutely bottomless. My learning and occasional moments of enlightenment continue to surprise and humble me. As hard as it is, I could not wish for a better teacher or profession.

When teaching a residential writing retreat in the U.K. recently, I spontaneously held up a blank sheet of paper and said, "This is my homeland."

This is my homeland.

Like all homelands, as soon as I assume that I know it, I discover that I don't know it.

This homeland compels me to be fully alert to each step I take or do not take in its territory, while simultaneously offering me endless possibilities.

I began this essay with a quote from "Page" that stunned me when I first wrote it:

"Between page and writer is a magnetism more compelling than any other relationship."

It stuns me still.

Acknowledgements

Every book has a story of how it became a story. When writing narrative, particularly fiction, this is referred to as the backstory — the story that a writer needs to know regarding the circumstances informing the narrative that are not apparent to the reader.

Breathing the Page: Reading the Act of Writing quite simply would never have existed without the initial inspiration of two essays I encountered as a young poet: Phyllis Webb's "On the Line" (*Talking*, 1982) and Margaret Atwood's "The Page" (*Murder in the Dark*, 1983). Webb's and Atwood's essays evoked a state of consciousness about the act of writing that elated me: opened a parallel, embodied world of thinking and writing about writing.

In 1984, Daphne Marlatt and I published our in-concert books *Touch to My Tongue* and *open is broken*. In these books we each pushed out the boundaries of the personal essay in the companion essays we wrote to accompany each of our collection of poems. It was then I got hooked on the essay form. By 1990 I had published my first collection of personal essays, *Proper Deafinitions*. A year later, an anthology of essays by Canadian and American authors that I initiated and edited, *In Versions: Writing by Dykes, Queers & Lesbians*, was published.

During my appointment with the Saskatoon Public Library as their Writer in Residence (1993–1994), I began my quest for an auxiliary language to use in conversation with the wide range of writers and authors with whom I did consults — a language that articulated the forces we inevitably struggle with that dwell below the language of craft.

In 1998, shortly after my son was born, I began my essays about the materials with which we work, and upon which we depend as writers, for I had discovered that an increased awareness about our

Acknowledgements

material invigorated our writing. Here I want to thank *The Capilano Review* editors Bob Sherrin and Ryan Knighton, who took a chance with these first, quirky essays and published "Alphabet," "Form — Poetry" (later "Nose to Nose"), and "A Word" in 1999. This spurred me on when I was tempted to think of these odd essays as just a tangent.

I continued writing, and began to include my essays on our working materials in courses and workshops I was teaching. Simultaneously, I continued to develop concepts and vocabulary for the forces beneath craft and found myself using these concepts more and more in my teaching and manuscript consulting. While on faculty at Sage Hill Summer Experience in Saskatchewan, my 2002 workshop students urged me to write an accompanying set of essays on the concepts with which I was teaching. They wanted to have them in hand and generously offered to help me if I needed any assistance to make this possible. Thus, I am indebted to them for spurring me on.

Later that year I began writing the concept essays, and between 2003 and 2004, my former student Sarah Leavitt helped me organize what was then feeling like an unwieldy project. Although I want to particularly mention the two programs I have enjoyed the most in-depth teaching experiences, The Writer's Studio at Simon Fraser University and Vancouver Manuscript Intensive, I am indebted to all the students who have trusted me with their writing. Indebted to all the writers and authors with whom I have done manuscript consults and editing. It is you who have sourced this book.

All the writing examples throughout the book are excerpts from my formers students' work (except those taken from mine). I am happy to be in such good company.

breathing

Over the past six years I have had the invaluable assistance of three editors: Lori McNulty, Barbara Kuhne, and Carol Murray. Barbara Kuhne's steady belief in *Breathing the Page: Reading the Act of Writing* has been vital, as has the enthusiasm of writer-editor and friend Lise Weil. Editor and Publisher Patrick Crean's support kept me going during the five long years of seeking a publisher. His respect for the manuscript buoyed me at some very crucial times. The authors of a number of books on writing have also companioned me during the twelve years I worked on this book. Many are quoted in the essays and/or are mentioned in Sources and Resources section.

Four remarkable books on writing have been my cornerstones. Three were published between 1927 and 1938: E.M. Forster's *Aspect of the Novel*, Brenda Ueland's *If You Want to Write*, and Dorothea Brande's *Becoming a Writer*. The fourth book, Virginia Woolf's posthumously published *A Writer's Diary*, is comprised of diary excerpts from 1918 to 1941 about her writing life. These four books are still among the most insightful books on writing in the English-speaking world.

Now, you hold *Breathing the Page: Reading the Act of Writing* in your hands, thanks to my spirited and insightful publisher and editor Marc Côté of Cormorant Books. Marc, you have my gratitude for believing this book into being.

I thank you each and all.

Sources and Resources

Abrams, David. *The Spell of the Sensuous: Perception and Language in a More-Than-Human World*. New York: Pantheon Books, 1996.

Brande, Dorothea. *Becoming A Writer*. New York: Putnam-Penguin, [1934], 1981.

Brandt, Di. Winnipeg. *questions I asked my mother*. Winnipeg: Turnstone Press, 1987.

Brook, Ian, Editor-in-Chief. *The Chambers Dictionary*. Edinburgh: Chambers Harrap Publishers Ltd., 2003.

Brossard, Nicole. *The Aerial Letter*. Toronto: The Women's Press, 1988.

Brossard, Nicole. Toronto. *Fluid Arguments*. Toronto: The Mercury Press, 2005.

Cixous, Hélène. *Coming to Writing and Other Essays*. Cambridge and London: Harvard University Press, 1991.

Cixous, Hélène. *Three Steps on the Ladder to Writing*. New York: Columbia University Press, 1993.

Forster, E.M. *Aspects of the Novel*. New York: Harcourt, Brace and Company, 1927.

Gluck, Louise. *Proofs and Theories: Essays on Poetry*. New York: The Ecco Press, An Imprint of HarperCollins Publishers, 1999.

Gunnars, Kristjana. *Stranger at the Door: Writers and the Act of Writing*. Waterloo: Wilfrid Laurier University Press, 2004.

Hampl, Patricia. *I Could Tell You Stories: Sojourns in the Land of Memory*. New York and London: W.W. Norton & Company, 1999.

Jabès, Edmond. *The Book of Questions*. Middletown: Wesleyan University Press, 1976.

Kincaid, Jamaica. *The Autobiography of My Mother*. New York: Farrar Straus Giroux, 1996.

Lee, Dennis. *Body Music*. Toronto: Anansi, 1998.

Levertov, Denise. *New & Selected Essays*. New York: A New Directions Book, 1992.

Marlatt, Daphne. *Touch to My Tongue*. Edmonton: Longspoon Press, 1984.

Maso, Carole. *Break Every Rule: Essays on Language, Longing & Moments of Desire*. Washington, D.C.: Counterpoint, 2000.

Morris, William, ed. *The American Heritage Dictionary of the English Language*. Boston: Houghton Mifflin Company, 1981.

Paré, Arleen. *Paper Trail*. Edmonton: NeWest Press, 2007.

Scarry, Elaine. *On Beauty and Being Just*. Princeton: Princeton University Press, 1999.

Stone, Anne. *delible*. Toronto: Insomniac Press, 2007.

Toews, Miriam. *a complicated kindness*. Toronto: Vintage Canada-Random House, 2004.

Ueland, Brenda. *If You Want to Write*. Saint Paul: Graywolf Press, [1938], 1987.

Woolf, Virginia. *A Room of One's Own*. Harmondsworth, Middlesex: Penguin Books Ltd., 1974.

Woolf, Virginia. *A Writer's Diary*. Frogmore, St Albans: Triad/Panther Books, [1953], 1979.

Webb, Phyllis. *Nothing But Brush Strokes*. Edmonton: NeWest Press, 1995.

Van der Pol, Astrid. *Invisible Lines*. Ottawa: Buschekbooks, 2003.

McLuhan, Marshall. *Counterblast*. Toronto: McClelland and Stewart Limited, 1969.

Sources and Resources

Milosz, Czeslaw. *The Witness of Poetry*. Cambridge and London: Harvard University Press, 1983.

breathing

Other Books by the Author

only this blue (long poem and essay). Toronto: The Mercury Press, 2005.

Bloodroot: Tracing the Untelling of Motherloss (memoir). Toronto: Sumach Press, 2000.

What Holds Us Here (poetry). Ottawa: Buschek Books, 1998.

Two Women in a Birth (poetry and prose with Daphne Marlatt). Toronto: Guernica Editions, 1994.

The Bat Had Blue Eyes (poetry and prose). Toronto: Women's Press, 1993.

Proper Deafinitions (essays). Vancouver: Press Gang Publishers, 1990.

Double Negative (poetry and prose with Daphne Marlatt). Charlottetown: gynergy books/Ragweed Press, 1988.

serpent (w)rite: a reader's gloss (a long poem). Toronto: Coach House Press, 1987.

open is broken (poetry). Edmonton: Longspoon Press, 1984.

A Gathering Instinct (poetry). Toronto: Williams-Wallace, 1981.

Publication History of Essays

"Alphabet," "Form — Poetry" (later re-titled "Nose to Nose"), "A Word" originally appeared in *The Capilano Review*, Vancouver, Series 2, No. 29, Fall 1999.

"The Pencil" originally appeared on www.betsywarland.com in 2004.

"Nose to Nose" appeared in my book *only this blue*, Mercury Press, Toronto, 2005, and in an abbreviated form in *Rocksalt: An Anthology of Contemporary BC Poetry*, Salt Spring Island, BC: Mother Tongue Publishing Limited, 2008, edited by Mona Fertig and Harold Rhenisch.

"The Computer" originally appeared in *Matrix*, Montreal, Issue 79, Spring 2008.

"Scored Space" originally appeared in the online zine *17 seconds*, Fall 2008.

"The Table" and "The Line" originally appeared in *Grain*, Saskatoon, Volume 36, Number 4, Summer 2009.

"Sustaining Yourself as a Writer" originally appeared on <www.betsy warland.com> in the fall of 2009.

"Memory as Metaphor" originally appeared in EVENT, Vancouver, issue 39/1, spring 2010.

breathing

Index of Writing Exercises

"Locating the Reader"
Assessing First Pages of Books, 6–7

"Embodiment"
Using the Three Preparatory Inscription Stages, 31–3
Developing Your Third Ear, 34–5
Assessment of Your Narrative via Scanning Your Body

"The Coma Story and the Comma Story"
Writing into the Comma in a Coma Story, 47–8

"Proximity"
The Burning House Exercise, 51–2
Adjusting to Proximity, 54–5

"Scaffolding"
Identifying Scaffolding, 66–8

"Depth of Field"
Changing Focus to Increase Depth of Field, 73

"Scored Space"
Writing into the Negative Space of Your Narrative, 80–1

"Spatiotemporal Structural Strategies"
How You Occupy Public Space Diagram, 89–91

"Intrinsic Form"
The Word or Phrase for How Your Narrative Constitutes
    and Expresses Itself, 119
Checking Your Accuracy of Form by Using Your Breath, 121
Collaborating with the Narrative to Re-score it in Three
    Different Ways, 123–4

"Territory and Landmarks"
Assessing Your Entire Narrative Visually, 128
Reconsidering the Narrative's Tangents, 129–30
Tracking the Role of Landmarks and Points of Intensification in
    Your Narrative, 130

"Sustaining Yourself as a Writer"
Concentric Circles Diagram and Questions, 161

breathing

Index of Terms, Phrases, and Images

Accuracy, 19, 78, 110

Additive writer, 85–7

Alphabet, 39–42, 108, 110, 167

Approach — Retreat — Return, 53, 72

Autobiographically based, 18, 19, 26, 43, 122, 136

Autobiographically generated, 18, 19, 26, 43

Authorized version, 17, 18

Baseline, 112

Bat Had Blue Eyes, The, 20, 66, 136

Blank sheet of paper (public space, homeland), 164–5

Bloodroot: Tracing the Untelling of Motherloss, 44, 83, 107, 137, 141

Blank space, 78–81, 98, 105

Billboarding, 6, 65

Body, 30, 31, 35–37, 40, 49, 110, 113, 123

Breath, breathing exercise, 41–2, 113, 121

Burning House (proximity), 51–2

Collaboration, 15

Coma story, 43–8, 73, 132

Commentary, 6, 65, 130

Community, 43, 65, 78, 91, 97, 134, 143, 154, 156–7

Companionship, 139, 143, 152, 154–7, 162

Compose/composition, 11, 24, 25, 27, 34, 35, 37, 49, 58, 61, 69, 83, 85–7, 91, 93, 101–2, 105, 114–5, 121, 139

Compositional strategies, 49, 69, 91, 93, 101–2

Compression, 93–4

Concentric Circles exercise, 161–3

Cones of fiction and creative non-fiction, 8–9

Containment, 91–3, 95

Context, 14, 15, 19, 22, 58, 61, 62, 70, 71, 80, 82, 89, 109, 118

Contiguity, 96–7

Contraction (and expansion), 99–100

Creative non-fiction, ix, 7–9, 36, 151

Crossing the threshold, 32, 149

Cueing the reader, 1, 6, 20, 55, 62, 82, 88, 89, 123, 131

Decoding, 46

Depth of field, 70–4, 101

Detachment, 37, 44, 51

Dimensions: 2-D and 3-D, 45, 88

Dog metaphors, 1, 3, 29, 38, 66, 76, 90, 108, 150

Drafts, ix, 6, 31, 54, 57, 64, 69, 73, 83, 105, 106, 122–8, 136, 137

Encodement, 64–5

Embodiment, 30–8, 76, 115n, 125

Index of Terms, Phrases, and Images

Excess and fixed points, 101–2
Explanatory, 106
Expansion, 95, 99–100
Explicit form, 117, 118, 124
Extension, 95

Fiction, ix, 7–9, 18, 47, 119
Fidelity to experience, 44, 120–1
First reader, ix, 66, 83, 129
Fixed points and excess, 101–2
Flat and round characters, 105
Focus, 8, 26, 30–2, 35, 36, 59, 66,
   70, 72, 85, 90, 92, 105, 118,
   121, 124–6, 131, 146, 152,
   154–6
Form, 30, 33, 37, 43, 45, 49, 50–61,
   87, 91, 98, 112, 115n, 117–
   27, 143
Forster, E.M., 15, 25, 95, 105, 168
Four *Ps*, l, 59

Habits of inscription, 26–7, 137

Image, 1, 59, 66, 80, 105, 117, 126,
   131
Incremental, 37–8, 53, 79, 86
Incognito, 153
Integrity, 13, 19, 110, 115, 123
Intensification, 93, 130–2
Interdependency, 29, 62, 109–10
Intrinsic (form, meaning), 117–27
Inscription, ix, 10, 24, 27, 32–7,
   57–61, 64, 69, 79, 85–7, 88,
   102, 105, 121, 124, 130, 136,
   137, 146, 147, 149

Juxtaposition, 47, 56, 129

Language, 16, 17, 30, 32, 34, 41,
   52, 58–60, 74, 76, 79–80, 82,
   88, 91, 105, 108, 111–4, 136,
   139–40
Levertov, Denise, 44, 120, 172
Listening, 34–5, 111, 139
Lived experience, 6, 7, 16, 19, 22,
   30, 43, 59, 74, 93, 155

Magnetism, 10, 144, 166
Meaning, 15, 34, 43, 52, 60, 61,
   62, 70, 79, 81, 84, 89, 104,
   108, 109, 113, 114, 120, 123,
   131, 144
Memory, 7, 14–20, 40, 45, 65, 110,
   114, 120–4, 136, 150

Narrative triangle, 15
Negative space, 79–81
Nuance, 53, 95, 133

only this blue, 44, 55, 95, 126

Pacing, 6, 58, 59, 83, 99, 101
Page, the, 9–12, 22
   as public space, 89–91
Pattern, 37, 59, 91, 106, 112, 120,
   123, 128, 136, 141

Perspectives, 5, 8, 18, 20, 43, 96,
    130, 148
Poetry, 11, 20, 22, 25, 30, 36,
    37, 45, 51, 60, 80, 87, 95,
    98, 112–6, 124, 126,
    128
Points of intensification (*see*
    Intensification)
Predicament, 1–2, 5, 6, 59, 91
Predilection, 2
Preparatory time/stages to write,
    31–2, 149–50, 152
Proximity, 26–7, 41, 51–9, 65, 70,
    73–4, 137
Publishing (publishers, self-
    publishing, websites, new
    media), 76, 83, 110, 135, 139,
    144–6, 151, 155–62

Reader's resistance, 5–6, 156

Scaffolding, 48, 57, 64–9
Scanning, 35
Scene of the accident, 18–20
Scored space, 22–3, 79–85, 113–4,
    118
serpent (w)rite — a reader's gloss,
    97, 135
Signature, 22, 36, 49, 50, 62, 69,
    90, 93, 102
Silence, 13, 18, 78, 82, 84, 114

Space, 22–3, 48, 59, 78–85, 89,
    113–4, 118
Space for the reader (and public
    space), 89–91
Spatial relationships, 55
Spatiotemporal, 49, 88–102
Something missing, 46
State of consciousness, 6, 26, 27,
    32, 35, 36, 57, 88
Structural strategies, 49, 88–102
Subtractive writer, 85–7

Tangent, 45, 47, 66, 129, 167
Template, 15, 45, 48, 75, 90, 124
Territory, 48, 85, 128–32, 166
Third ear, 35, 156
Timing, 88, 109, 133
Tone, 35, 52, 58, 65, 70, 73, 83,
    83, 88, 109, 112, 113, 156
Tree metaphors, 24–6, 28, 75, 76,
    162
True story, 17, 20
Truth, 9, 16, 20, 76, 107, 123

Vacuity, 98–8

Waiting, 98–9
Website, 32, 137
Woolf, Virginia, 31, 38, 93, 94n,
    122, 140, 141

breathing